H. Wayne Fink

D0122607

2/79

THE DAILY STUDY BIBLE SERIES
REVISED EDITION

WILLIAM BARCLAY

INDEX VOLUME

Edited by C. L. Rawlins

THE WESTMINSTER PRESS
PHILADELPHIA

Published by The Westminster Press®
Philadelphia, Pennsylvania

PRINTED IN THE UNITED STATES OF AMERICA

9   8   7   6   5   4   3   2   1

Library of Congress Cataloging in Publication Data

Rawlins, C   L
    The Daily study Bible, revised edition [by] William
Barclay. : an index volume.

    Index to the Daily study Bible series, rev. ed.
    1. The Daily study Bible series — Indexes.
I. Barclay, William, lecturer in the University of
Glasgow. II. Title.
BS2341.2.R38   220.7′016   78-18316
ISBN 0-664-21370-7
ISBN 0-664-24215-4 pbk.

CONTENTS

INTRODUCTION

The Daily Study Bible hardly needs an introduction. Since its inception twenty five years ago, 'the little red commentaries'[1] have circulated in their thousands around the world and are to be found from archbishops' palaces to the more humble homes of ordinary people on five continents.

It was in the year of the Coronation that the then relatively unknown lecturer in New Testament studies at the University of Glasgow provided, at short notice, his first commentary; there was no indication then that it would be the precursor of a full series or that it would be selling on a world-wide scale a quarter of a century later. But so it was, and within six years it was complete—an extraordinary event which even pre-planned series with multiple authors and the full backing of fully staffed publishing houses has not equalled. And so the name of William Barclay became an household name with more than sixty books to his credit, countless articles in periodicals both popular and technical, and radio and television appearances which attracted record listening and viewing.[2]

And what is the DSB (as it is familiarly called)? Precisely what its title asserts: a *daily* study of the Bible. It is not just a commentary, if by that term one implies full critical and exegetical treatment of the text, nor if one understands it to mean a fully-worked exposition. To be sure, these matters are not excluded from these studies, and behind them there lies a masterful comprehension of biblical learning, as his other works show.[3] But in this series we have Barclay the pastor rather than Barclay the Professor of Divinity and Biblical Criticism, an important aspect which several critics have over-looked when they have spoken of the unevenness of treatment in this or that part. As the author himself declares, in setting out his aims in the General Introduction, it is 'to make the results of modern scholarship available to the non-technical reader in a form that does not require a theological education to understand; and then to make the teaching of the New Testament books relevant to life and work today . . . they are meant to enable men and women to know Jesus Christ more clearly, to love him more dearly, and to follow him more nearly'.[4]

In other words, the books (seventeen in all, extending over more than four thousand pages) provide us with exposition which is informative, devotional and relevant, as any *daily* encounter with the scriptures should be. And how informative! For those with the inclination and discipline to take them seriously they are a veritable gold-mine. In these practiced hands the world of the New Testament comes vibrantly alive, alive with the authentic ring of first-hand experience and the touch of the craftsman-writer. Through these pages we are introduced to the air breathed by the early Christians, made to sit where they sat, and helped to see things as they saw them. The message to them thus becomes the message to us, for Dr Barclay is a most practical writer, a pastor *par excellence*. Ever ready to enlighten and enliven the most casual reference or mundane comment, his main task is to home-in on the real meaning and present-day reality of the passage under consideration. As he says himself, 'Christianity is truth, but it is truth in action'.[5] Relevance might be his second name. But how devotional, too! In some commentators' hands the Bible is handled with clinical precision: introduced, analysed, explained —and the net result is a descriptive piece which would grace any museum. . . . Barclay is not such a writer. His work radiates an infectious love for Christ and mankind, and thus through his books there develops a powerful encounter between both. But it is an encounter, and his ethic is one, therefore, of 'reciprocal obligation',[6] towards God and man.

In all this he is clear and frank. Where there are problems he says so; where there are difficulties he admits them; where there are discrepancies, weaknesses, contradictions even, he states them, fully and carefully. If a statement conflicts with present-day modes of thought or practice he does not baulk the issue or weaken his stance; the reader is left always in a position to be responsive to God and his Word. The whole thrust of his exposition is to bring the would-be Christian under the inexorable demands of Christ, demands which are humbling and demanding in a total sense, as Barclay is at pains to declare.

He does not dilute the reality of sin, the danger of compromise or the existence of God's wrath; nor does he obscure the glorious reality of his love and kindness, his willingness to forgive and heal, his power to deliver from enslaving habits, and the hope he inspires. All these, and much more, are found finely stated and illustrated in these commentaries. His exposition is carefully balanced, more so than many—whether 'liberal' or 'conservative'—are prepared to admit. These, with his simplicity and directness of style,[7] are some of the reasons for his great success and usefulness.[8]

This *Index* is simply an aid to the greater and more effective use of the preceding seventeen books. Its format demonstrates the method and strengths of Barclay the commentator. He is primarily a *biblical* theologian. Not only in the sense that his life and energies have been spent in the service of the Bible, by studies linguistic and archaeological, exegetical and practical, classical and modern, but also in the sense that he allows the Bible to create its own theological ethos, dictate its own theological style, provide its own theological language, direct, in a word, its own theological ends. The interpretive rules (or hermeneutic) he uses are themselves biblically oriented. He is not a manipulator of scripture, but one manipulated by it; his authority is of one 'under authority'.[9] In all his writings the axiom of scripture interpreting scripture predominates. In this way he preserves the integrity of scripture and the inter-relatedness of its several parts.

Any commentator of whole books of the Bible is placed under the severe discipline of facing unavoidably a wide range of subjects and problems. The second section of this *Index* manifests Barclay's ability to grapple with major and contentious issues fairly and competently. He is not evasive, but brings all matters under the searchlight of the full biblical revelation and record, whether they be matters of the moment or ones of more lasting consequence, personal or public.

Nor does he work in isolation from contemporary scholars or those of past ages. In the third section his indebtedness to their knowledge and experience (never divorced!) is shown. Thanks to great industry, wide reading and a phenomenal memory,[10] his works are replete with quotations and anecdotes of all sorts: practical, philosophical, religious, secular, antiquarian, modern, prose, poetry, and in several languages. From the Hebrides to the Antipodes he draws from a rich fund which never fails to interest or inform. In the final two sections of the *Index* we see much of the sources of Dr Barclay's exposition. Here etymology and ancient practice join hands in a creative act of enlightenment of scripture which could otherwise remain meaningless to the modern reader.

Users of this *Index* should be aware of the 'chain-reference' method whereby they can trace a great deal of information about the subject of their enquiry from small beginnings. In a writer of Barclay's stature this is particularly important, for his use of language is rich and fluent; he moves swiftly through adjectives and synonyms.[11] I have not sought to centralize subjects under single heads, so readers should be alive to a fairly diverse form of reference. For example, those wishing to understand his emphasis on right doctrine should refer to 'Doctrine', 'Belief', 'The Faith', 'Creeds', and 'Orthodoxy'. Further aspects may be explored in other sections, such as under Personal Names (e.g. Jesus or Paul), key scripture references (e.g. Rom. 3:21-25 for 'justification'), or foreign words; by this method the user will be enabled to reach a comprehensive viewpoint of Dr Barclay's thought.

This volume is sent out with the prayer that it may be found to be a worthy servant of the series and the One to whom the whole series looks as both Lord and Master.

A number of people have helped in various ways, to whom I record my deep appreciation and gratitude: Mr Tim Honeyman (Secretary of the Church of Scotland Publications Committee) and Mr Maurice Berrill (its former Publisher) have both supplied much help and encouragement notwithstanding some delays; Mrs Beryl Barnes produced an admirable typescript from a difficult manuscript; my wife Veronica willingly shouldered many extra jobs in addition to her professional and domestic tasks; but above all to Dr Barclay himself whose tireless efforts bring to us the ripe fruits of learning year after year.

C. L. RAWLINS

Postscript

Some months after the above was written, news reached me of the death of Dr Barclay. He had seen it, and it had met with his approval, but the Foreword he had promised remains unwritten.

From around the world there has come a flow of appreciations for this great man, undoubtedly one of the foremost communicators of the Christian faith of the century. They will continue, as his work will continue, for it is based on the unchanging expression of God's will and purposes in Christ Jesus. Let this small volume stand as part of the living memorial in William Barclay's honour, who counted not the praise of men but only of God himself.

C. L. R.

NOTES

1. They were revised and reset in 1974–76.
2. See 'Barclay the Broadcaster' by the late Ronald Falconer, in *Biblical Studies: Essays in Honour of William Barclay*, edited by J. R. McKay and J. F. Miller (William Collins & Sons, 1976, pp. 15–27).
3. See the 'Table of Events and Selected Works' in *Men and Affairs* (A. R. Mowbray & Co., pp. 147–149).
4. Richard of Chichester's prayer is quoted in the General Introduction to both the original and the revised editions of the series.
5. 12.100, a passage which particularly emphasizes the need for Christian action.

6. See, for example, **11**.160f. Dr Barclay twice uses this phrase in the DSB, but the concept pervades the whole of his thought both ethically and theologically.
7. See the Editor's Preface in *Men and Affairs*, pp. viiif.
8. David Edwards, formerly one of Dr Barclay's editors but now Dean of Westminster Abbey, refers to this in the Preface to *Testament of Faith* (A. R. Mowbray & Co., 1975, pp. vii–xii).
9. Matt. 8:9; significantly, Barclay finds the centurion who originally voiced these words 'one of the most attractive characters in the gospels' (**1**.300). Johnston McKay and James Miller, in the Editors' Preface to *Biblical Studies*, refer (somewhat clumsily) to Barclay's 'biblicality' (p.9).
10. See Dr Barclay's modest admission of this in *Testament of Faith* (p. 22f.); David Edwards highlights it in his Preface (p. viii).
11. Note Edwards' reference to this as 'his extraordinary appetite for words' (op. cit., p. ix).

EXPLANATION OF USE

For reasons of space the seventeen volumes of the *Daily Study Bible* have each been given a numerical reference (1–17); these references are printed in *bold type* throughout the book; the key to these will be found at the foot of every page. The main exposition of a passage is printed in italics, thus references to Philippians 3:1 will appear as: **11**.7, 15, *50–53*; **14**.336. It will be found that volume **11** is *Philippians, Colossians and Thessalonians* and volume **14** is *James and Peter*; the primary passage will be found at pages 50–53 of the former volume.

INDEX OF OLD TESTAMENT REFERENCES

12:8	2.245; 3.273; 4.24; 6.10	20:7	14.188; 15.29
13–14	4.58	20:10	1.146; 6.2
13	3.44	20:14	17.149
13:45–46	1.296, 365; 4.58, 218	20:21	3.150
13:47–52	15.205	20:26	11.11; 14.188; 15.29
13:47	3.44	21:6	11.10
14	1.299; 3.45	21:9	17.149
14:1–7	14.170	21:16–23	13.78
14:22	2.245; 3.273	23:10–11	3.323; 9.150
14:33	3.44	23:21	7.21
15:14	2.245; 3.273	23:27–32	13.101
15:19–33	4.113	23:39	5.248
15:25–27	1.346; 3.129	23:40	5.249
15:29	2.245	24:5–9	2.23; 4.70
16	13.97, 101	24:9	3.63
16:4	14.107; 16.45	24:16	3.49; 6.76, 234
16:12	17.40	24:19–20	1.163
16:15	13.103	25:23	5.59
16:19	6.77	25:39–42	6.23
16:21–22	13.103	26:5	5.168
16:27	13.197	26:11–12	9.223; 17.203
16:29	13.98	26:21–26	17.9
16:31	1.233	26:26	17.7
16:32	15.69	26:41	11.55, 139
16:33	13.98	27:30	2.293; 11.10
17:11–14	17.10	27:32	6.56; 11.10
17:11	13.107		
18:5	8.138		
18:8	9.44	***Numbers***	
18:16	3.150		
19:2	14.188; 15.29	4:3	6.36
19:9	2.16	5:2	4.218
19:13	14.118	5:6–7	1.57
19:15	14.63	5:7	4.235
19:18	1.165; 2.278; 3.295; 4.140; 14.111; 15.44	6:1–21	7.138; 12.119
		6:22–27	16.135
19:23–25	3.282	8:4	17.10
20:5	1.330	9:12	6.261
		9:15	17.121

Deuteronomy

2:24	8.124	12:9	13.33
3:6	8.124	13:1–5	6.48; **14.**315, 319;
3:9	1.260		**14.**89; **17.**131
3:24	14.271	13:6	5.74; 7.61
4:2	17.231	13:8–11	8.124
4:11	13.185	13:13	9.104; **11.**212
4:12	5.73, 197	14:1	8.124
4:23	13.91	14:2	5.59; **14.**166
4:24	13.189	14:21	2.112
4:34	14.42	14:22	2.293; **4.**224
5:23–27	13.185	15:4	14.173
5:32–33	6.157	15:7–11	1.169; **9.**235
6:4–9	1.192; 2.286; 3.295;	15:9	1.246
	4.140; **17.**99	15:11	3.326; **6.**113
6:4	3.295; 4.140; 8.60;	15:23	5.224
	9.252	16:13–16	5.248
6:5	2.278	17:2–7	13.124
6:8	2.286; 3.295	17:6	5.195; 6.14; **15.**112
6:13	1.70; **4.**44	17:7	6.234; **9.**48
6:16	1.69; **4.**44	17:12	13.46
7:6	5.59; **14.**166	18:3–4	2,17
7:13	17.6	18:15	2.9; 4.115; 5.78, 206,
7:19	14.42		252; **6.**72
8:3	1.68; **4.**43	18:18	5.206, 252; 6.72;
8:8	2.251		**17.**71
9:3	5.30	18:20	14.315
9:19	13.186	19:10	14.173
9:26	14.271	19:15	2.188; 5.195; 6.13;
9:27	14.35		**15.**112; **17.**70
9:29	14.267	19:18	1.164
10:12	9.207	19:19	9.221
10:16	11.55	19:21	1.163
10:20	4.44	21:1–9	2.362
11:4–9	3.295	21:3	2.239; **3.**266
11:13–21	1.192; 2.286; 3.295;	21:17	4.204
	4.140; **17.**99	21:19	2.143
11:13	4.140	21:22–23	2.372; **6.**260
11:14	14.121; **17.**6	21:23	7.27; 9.17; **10.**26
11:18	2.286	22:10	9.221

1 Matt, v.1	**3** Mark	**5** John, v.1	**7** Acts	**9** Cor
2 Matt, v.2	**4** Luke	**6** John, v.2	**8** Rom	**10** Gal, Eph

22:12	1.347; 2.286; 4.113
22:13–24	6.2
23:3	1.17
23:18	11.54; 17.227
23:21–22	1.159
23:24–25	2.253
23:25	2.21; 3.63; 4.69
24:1	1.151; 2.197, 200; 3.238–40; 4.211
24:5	4.194
24:7	9.48
24:14–15	14.118
24:19	2.16
25:1–3	9.253
25:4	9.79; 12.116
25:5–10	2.277; 3.289
25:5–6	4.41, 249
25:7	2.143; 14.263
26:18	5.59
27:4	5.157
27:14–26	11.142
27:26	10.26, 30
28:6	6.59
28:35	17.126
28:51	17.6
29:4	8.145
29:17–18	17.44
29:18	13.182
29:23	15.185
29:28	14.37
30:6	11.55, 139
30:12–13	8.138
30:14	14.57
30:15–20	1.278; 5.146
30:19	16.109
31:16	2.276; 5.143; 14.102; 16.108; 17.106
31:29	6.157
32:4	2.140

32:6	6.27; 8.124
32:8	15.183
32:9	5.59
32:11–12	17.85
32:15	12.18
32:16	14.104
32:21	8.122, 142; 14.104
32:31	2.140
32:32	15.185
32:35f	13.125
32:39	2.276; 5.186; 14.112
32:43	8.198; 13.19; 17.165
33:1	12.134
33:17	16.171
33:27	5.30
34:1–4	14.181
34:5–6	2.159; 6.90, 177
34:5	14.293

Joshua

1:2	8.12; 11.10; 12.227
1:5	13.194
2:1–21	13.161; 14.78
2:1–7	1.17
2:9–11	13.161
3:10	16.48; 17.22
3:17	17.128
5:14–15	13.17
6:1–20	13.160
6:17	8.124
6:25	13.161
7	8.79
7:1–26	8.124
7:19	6.48
7:21	1.239
9	1.73
9:6	13.90

10:11	**17**.134
14:7	**3**.281
19:28–29	**3**.178
24:15	**1**.278; **5**.146; **16**.109
24:29	**6**.178; **8**.12; **12**.227; **14**.35, 293; **16**.25
24:32	**5**.147; **13**.153

Judges

2:2	**13**.90
2:8	**11**.10; **16**.25
2:17	**17**.106
2:22	**14**.42
3:1, 4	**14**.42
4–5	**13**.163
4:4	**16**.105
5:14	**11**.58
5:19–21	**17**.132
5:31	**16**.51
6–7	**13**.163
6:49	**16**.25
7:21	**14**.115
8:23	**6**.236; **10**.108
8:27, 33	**17**.106
9:8–15	**3**.89
9:13	**12**.79
10:4	**6**.118
11–12	**13**.163
13–16	**13**.163
13:18	**17**.180
13:20	**13**.18
13:22	**10**.129
14:12	**14**.116
18:30	**17**.25
20:16	**6**.55
20:26	**1**.234

Ruth

1:4	**1**.17
1:22	**1**.24
2:14	**6**.146

1 Samuel

1	**13**.163
1:16	**17**.59
2:1–10	**4**.15
2:2	**2**.140; **17**.120
2:6	**5**.187; **14**.112
2:12	**17**.59
2:27	**12**.134
3:1–14	**6**.126
3:14	**2**.42
6:7	**2**.239
7:6	**1**.234
9:1–2	**11**.58
9:6	**12**.134
9:16	**15**.69
10:1	**15**.69
10:2	**1**.38
12:12	**6**.236
15:22	**3**.296; **13**.114
16:1–13	**13**.163
16:1	**1**.24; **16**.133
16:3, 12	**15**.69
16:13	**16**.133
17:12	**1**.24
17:34–36	**6**.61
18:4	**16**.46
20:6	**1**.24
21:1–6	**2**.23; **3**.63; **4**.70
22:2	**2**.140
23:14–15	**1**.24
23:18	**13**.90

1 Matt, v.1	**3** Mark	**5** John, v.1	**7** Acts	**9** Cor
2 Matt, v.2	**4** Luke	**6** John, v.2	**8** Rom	**10** Gal, Eph

24:5–11	**16**.46
24:14	**11**.54
25:17, 25	**17**, 59
26:21	**16**.65
28:14	**2**.276
29:4	**1**.225; **3**.22; **17**.81

2 Samuel

3:18	**3**.281; **14**.293
7:14	**3**.71; **9**.223; **13**.19; **17**.206
9:7, 13	**6**.142
10:4	**16**.143
11–12	**1**.17
12:1–14	**16**.145
12:1–13	**3**.50
12:1–7	**3**.85, 89
13:28–29	**12**.79
14:4	**3**.268
16:7	**17**.59
17:23	**6**.118
18:15	**13**.164
19:22	**1**.225; **3**.22
19:26	**6**.118
22:5	**11**.212
22:32	**2**.140

1 Kings

2:22	**16**.133
3:7	**6**.59
4:25	**2**.251; **5**.93
5:4	**1**.225; **3**.22; **17**.81
6:20	**17**.212

6:23–30	**16**.158
7:49	**16**.45
8:2	**5**.248
8:10–11	**2**.161; **3**.210; **14**.259; **17**.122, 203
8:11	**5**.69
8:17–18	**15**.87
8:18	**1**.101
8:53	**14**.35
8:66	**16**.25
11:14, 23	**17**.81
11:29–32	**2**.240; **3**.339; **4**.239; **7**.154; **13**.13
11:30–32	**3**.264
11:36	**16**.25
12:21	**11**.58
12:22	**12**.134
12:29	**17**.25
13:22	**17**.72
14:13	**16**.121
16:31	**16**.105
17–18	**14**.132
17:1–7	**17**.79
17:1	**14**.132; **17**.42, 71
17:17ff	**13**.166
18	**6**.45
18:1	**14**.132
18:13	**16**.106
18:15	**17**.42
18:17–40	**1**.64
18:19	**6**.143; **16**.106
18:26	**1**.196
18:37	**6**.100
18:42	**14**.132
19:1–8	**4**.126; **6**.126; **13**.164; **17**.79
19:3	**1**.64
19:4	**17**.143
19:8	**3**.22

19:9–12	**2.**159
19:10–18	**8.**144
19:11	**17.**20
19:12	**16.**50
19:13	**1.**281
19:15–16	**15.**69
19:19	**1.**281
20:8	**14.**263
20:35–43	**12.**102
21	**16.**106
21:10	**11.**212; **17.**59
21:11	**14.**263
21:13	**11.**212; **17.**59
22	**14.**314f
22:11	**16.**171
22:19	**13.**17; **16.**151, 153

2 Kings

1:8	**1.**44, 282; **3.**16
1:9–10	**17.**71
2:11	**2.**159; **17.**70, 72
2:12	**2.**287
3:14	**17.**42
4:8ff	**13.**166
4:18–37	**4.**86
4:29	**4.**134
5	**3.**127
5:5	**14.**116
5:6	**5.**186; **17.**42
5:7	**14.**112
5:22	**1.**239; **14.**116
6:17	**3.**24
6:26	**3.**268
6:31ff	**13.**164
6:32	**14.**263
7:3–3	**1.**365

8:13	**11.**54
9:13	**2.**239; **3.**266
9:22	**16.**106
9:27	**17.**132
9:36	**16.**25
10:10	**16.**25
15:5	**1.**365
17:6	**5.**149
17:23	**14.**37
17:24	**5.**149
17:28	**5.**159
17:29	**5.**157, 159
18:4	**5.**134
18:17–37	**17.**22
19:15	**16.**158
19:34	**16.**25
19:35–36	**12.**150; **13.**18
20:1–7	**13.**164
20:6	**16.**25
20:20	**6.**43
21:1–9	**9.**221
21:10	**16.**25
22:14	**16.**105
23:3ff	**9.**221
23:10	**1.**141; **3.**231
23:29–30	**17.**132
24:14–16	**14.**37
25:26	**14.**39

1 Chronicles

5:26	**14.**37
9:33	**17.**34
17:4	**16.**25
21:1	**17.**59
24:5, 7–18	**16.**153
29:10–12	**16.**179

---

1 Matt, v.1	**3** Mark	**5** John, v.1	**7** Acts	**9** Cor
2 Matt, v.2	**4** Luke	**6** John, v.2	**8** Rom	**10** Gal, Eph

19:25	**14.125**	8:2	**2.249**
21:20	**17.111**	8:4–6	**13.23**
22:29	**14.109**	8:4	**2.26**
23:3	**3.25**	8:5	**13.24**
25:4	**4.13**	8:6–8	**14.89**
26:6	**17.51**	9:10	**1.205; 4.143; 5.62;**
26:13	**15.62**		**6.210; 15.53**
27:9	**6.48**	9:13	**16.52**
28:17	**16.156**	9:18	**1.91**
28:19	**17.214**	10:7	**8.55**
28:22	**17.51**	14:1–3	**8.55**
28:28	**9.207**	14:1	**1.140; 3.314f**
29:3	**6.13**	15	**3.293**
31:12	**17.51**	15:3	**1.274**
33:4	**1.22**	16:5	**14.174**
37:4	**16.155**	16:8–11	**14.181**
37:9–10	**17.20**	16:9–11	**6.92; 9.139**
38–41	**8.27**	16:10	**5.117**
38:7	**14.322**	16:11	**6.158**
38:31	**16.48**	18	**16.25**
40:15–24	**17.77**	18:2	**2.140**
42:7	**16.25**	18:10	**16.158**
42:12	**14.125**	18:15	**17.20**
		18:31	**2.140**
		18:49	**14.127**
		18:50	**8.198**
Psalms		19:1–2	**16.159**
1:1	**1.88**	19:4	**8.141**
2	**14.181**	19:9	**9.208**
2:2	**17.73, 132**	19:10	**17.57**
2:5	**10.18**	20:7	**1.206; 5.60f; 6.210;**
2:7	**1.60; 4.38; 13.19, 47**		**15.54**
2:8–9	**16.110**	21:3	**14.49**
2:8	**1.70**	22	**2.368; 12.220; 14.181**
2:9	**17.75, 78, 182**	22:7–8	**2.368**
5:9	**8.55**	22:16	**11.54**
6:5	**6.91; 9.138; 14.237;**	22:18	**2.368; 6.255**
	16.181	22:20	**11.54**
8	**13.23**	22:22	**6.210; 13.27**

69:9	5.114; 8.197; 11.60		89:3	11.10; 15.25
69:21	6.259		89:4	6.128
69:22–23	8.145		89:6	14.322
69:28	16.123; 17.196		89:10	15.62; 17.58
72:4	1.91		89:12	3.210
73:9	14.85		89:17	16.171
73:13	14.108		89:20ff	3.298; 6.178
73:23–26	14.174		89:20	11.10
73:23–24	3.292; 6.92; 9.139		89:27	11.119; 16.33; 17.206
73:27	5.143		90	12.134
74:12–14	17.77		90:4	3.108; 14.250, 342;
74:13	17.47			17.188
75:4	16.171		90:15	16.9; 17.188
75:8	3.255; 17.111		91:6	12.214
77:18	13.188; 16.155		91:7–10	1.181
77:20	6.53		91:11–12	1.69
78:1–3	2.69		92:5	17.119
78:24–25	16.95		94:11	9.34
78:24	5.215		94:12	14.246; 16.145
78:45	17.130		95:7–11	13.33, 37
78:70	11.10; 14.293		95:7	6.53
79:3	17.72		96:1	16.176
79:5–10	17.12		97:1	17.172
79:10	14.338		97:7	13.19
79:13	6.53		98:1	16.176; 17.119
80:1	6.53; 16.158; 17.38		98:2	17.120
80:8	6.172		98:5	16.174
82:6	6.77		99:1	16.158
83:13–14	14.85		99:3	17.120
83:13	17.20		100:3	6.53; 14.216
85:2	1.56		101:5	14.111
86:9	17.120		101:7	17.228
86:11	6.158		102:25–27	17.195
86:14–16	12.25		102:25–26	17.15
87:4	17.58		102:26–27	13.19
88:5	6.92		103:2	4.219; 17.28
88:10–12	6.92; 9.138; 14.237;		103:15	14.48
	16.181		103:22	16.159
88:11	17.51		104:2	16.122, 151; 17.75

1 Matt, v.1	**3** Mark	**5** John, v.1	**7** Acts	**9** Cor
2 Matt, v.2	**4** Luke	**6** John, v.2	**8** Rom	**10** Gal, Eph

104:3	**16**.155; **17**.54		118:6	**13**.194
104:4	**13**.19		118:22–23	**3**.283; **4**.247; **8**.135
104:30	**1**.22		118:22	**2**.264; **14**.194
105:6	**6**._5; **14**.166		118:25	**2**.239; **5**.249
105:26	**14**.293; **16**.25		118:26	**2**.2, 239; **3**.266
105:30	**17**.130		118:29	**5**.249
105:33	**2**.151		119:30	**6**.158
105:41	**5**.251		119:103	**17**.57
105:43	**14**.166		119:174	**14**.192
106:1	**17**.169		120–134	**3**.324
106:2	**1**.196		121:3	**15**.207
107:18	**16**.52		121:6	**3**.119
107:20	**5**.29		121:8	**6**.59
107:30	**5**.210		122	**3**.324
107:41	**1**.91		124:4	**3**.255; **17**.86
109:6	**17**.81		124:8	**15**.87
109:14	**6**.38		130:8	**1**.19
110	**14**.181		132:10	**16**.25
110:1	**2**.279; **3**.298; **4**.252;		132:15	**1**.91
	13.19		133:1	**11**.14; **14**.209
110:4	**13**.67, 71, 72, 80		135:1	**17**.169, 171
111:1	**17**.169		135:4	**5**.59
111:2	**17**.119		135:20	**17**.171
111:9	**17**.120		136	**1**.390; **2**.342; **3**.338
112:1	**17**.169		136:5–6	**5**.168
112:3	**9**.235		137	**14**.37
112:9	**9**.235; **16**.171		137:8	**17**.153
113–118	**2**.342; **3**.338; **5**.249;		139:1–4	**5**.163
	6.116; **17**.169		139:12	**17**.219
113–114	**3**.338		139:14	**17**.119
113:1	**17**.169		140:3	**8**.55
114:7	**13**.188		141:2	**16**.174
115–118	**3**.338		141:8	**6**.152
115:17	**6**.92; **9**.138; **14**.237		144:9	**16**.176
116:8	**9**.173		144:10	**16**.25
117:1	**8**.198; **17**.169		145:1	**10**.108
118	**3**.267		145:15	**1**.176
118:1	**5**.249		145:17	**17**.120
118:5–6	**6**.116		145:19	**6**.48f

35:12	14.63	
36:9	17.221	

Ecclesiastes

2:5	16.70
2:15–16	16.84
2:24	9.154
3:12	9.154
5:2	1.196
5:18	9.154
7:20	14.82
8:15	9.154
9:2	16.84
9:4–5	9.138; 16.84
9:7	3.38; 9.154
9:8	16.122
9:10	6.92; 9.138; 14.237

Song of Solomon

3:11	14.49
5:2–6	16.147
6:3	17.203
6:10	17.75
8:7	9.125

Isaiah

1:9–10	17.71
1:9	15.185
1:11–20	13.115
1:11–17	5.112
1:15	6.48; 12.65
1:16–17	12.256
1:16	1.54; 14.107

1:18	16.49; 17.30
1:21	17.142
1:30	16.70
2:2–4	17.216
2:2	15.59
2:4	16.10
2:12	7.25
3:9	15.185
3:16–17	17.154
3:18–24	14.221
4:3	17.196
5:1–7	3.281; 4.245; 6.172
5:7	2.261
5:8	14.117
6	13.17
6:1	16.151
6:3	5.69; 16.127, 162
6:4	17.122
6:5–6	14.107
6:5	10.102; 17.36
6:6	17.41
6:8	1.360; 8.12
6:9–13	8.145
6:9–10	2.68; 3.92; 4.99; 6.132; 8.145
7:3	8.145
8:12	8.145
8:7–8	17.137
8:13–15	2.265
8:13–14	14.195
8:13	14.229
8:14	8.135
8:17	13.27
8:18	8.145
9:1–2	1.75
9:2–7	3.298
9:7	3.193; 6.128
9:12	8.145
9:18	14.85

9:19	8.25	22:15–25	16.133
10:22–23	8.120, 133	22:22	2.145; 16.128
11:1–9	3.298	23	2.12
11:1	1.40; 3.193; 16.2, 170; 17.228	23:1, 14	14.115
		23:16–17	17.142
11:2	16.31, 116	24:21–22	14.237
11:4	16.51; 17.178, 182	24:21	17.47
11:6–9	3.24; 16.10	24:23	16.153; 17.47
11:10	8.198; 16.2, 170	25:6	17.174
11:12	17.19, 216	25:8	16.11; 17.203
11:13	16.10	26:1	17.210
11:16	17.128	26:3	1.261
12:3	5.154, 249	26:19	2.276
13:6–16	3.304; 7.25	27:1	15.62; 17.58, 77
13:6	14.115; 17.16	27:12	16.8
13:8	17.16	27:13	3.319; 17.42
13:9	4.257; 6.197; 8.25; 11.204; 14.344	28:1–2	14.49
		28:2	17.134
13:10–13	4.257; 14.344	28:7	14.315
13:10	2.303; 3.319; 16.7; 17.14	28:9–12	9.131
		28:16	2.265; 8.121, 135, 139; 14.194
13:13	2.303; 17.15		
13:19–22	16.8, 149	29:6	14.341
13:19	15.185	29:10	8.145
14:12	15.183; 16.111; 17.59, 80	29:13	3.167
		29:14	9.17
14:13	17.133	30:21	6.157
14:31	14.115	30:30	14.341
15:2–3	14.115	31:4	6.61
16:7	14.115	32:15	16.10
19:2	17.5	33:15	3.294
20:3–4	7.154; 14.36	33:18	9.17
20:3	16.25	33:24	16.11
20:4	16.143	34:4	3.319; 17.14, 15
20:7	14.293	34:8–10	17.112
21:9	17.111	34:9–10	17.170
22:5	11.204	34:11–15	17.150
22:9–11	6.43	35:1	16.10
22:14	2.42	35:5–6	6.72

55:11	1.369; 5.29	66:15	17.20
56:1	3.294	66:19	17.217
56:6–8	17.217	66:22	17.197
56:7	2.247; 3.274f	66:24	3.232
56:8	6.63		
56:11	3.178		
56:12	9.154		
57:15	14.110		
57:19	10.111		
58:11	5.250		
59:7–8	8.55	*Jeremiah*	
59:20–21	8.152	1:4–5	8.12
59:21	5.83	1:5	6.77, 216
60:10–20	17.201	2:2	16.63
60:12	1.304; 10.122	2:7	5.59; 14.173
60:14	16.130	2:13	5.154; 17.220
60:19–20	17.216	2:21	6.172
60:19	6.13	2:23	14.173
61	4.48	2:35	1.57
61:1	5.84; 15.69	3:2	14.173
61:2	15.36	3:6–11	2.49
61:6	16.35	3:6–10	17.76
62:2	16.99	3:14	17.172
62:5	9.246	3:17	17.217
63:1–3	17.181	3:18	16.10
63:3	17.116	3:20	14.101; 16.108
63:6	16.8	4:13	17.20
63:16	6.27	4:24	17.15
64:4	3.292	5:24	14.121
64:6	17.30	6:10	11.55, 139
64:8	6.27	6:14	1.281; 14.314
65:1	8.142	7:11	2.247; 3.274
65:6–7	6.38	7:22	5.112
65:14	14.115	7:25	3.281; 8.12; 11.10;
65:17	8.109; 17.197		12.227; 14.36
65:19	17.203	7:34	17.167
65:20–22	16.10	8:3	17.51
65:25	16.10	8:11	1.281
66:15–16	14.341; 16.7	8:13	2.251

11 Phil, Col, Thes	**13** Heb	**15** John, Jude	**16** Rev, v.1
12 Tim, Tit, Phlm	**14** Jas, Pet		**17** Rev, v.2

B

Lamentations

1:12	**6**.254
1:15	**17**.116
1:30	**1**.30
3:24	**14**.174
3:30	**1**.165
4:6	**15**.185
5:16	**14**.49
5:21	**12**.44

Ezekiel

1:6	**16**.157
1:7	**16**.50
1:10	**16**.157
1:13	**16**.155
1:18	**16**.157
1:22, 26	**16**.157
1:28	**5**.69; **16**.51; **17**.54
2:1	**8**.220
2:9–10	**16**.165
3:1, 3	**17**.57
3:12	**16**.43
3:14	**17**.143
3:15	**16**.39
3:18	**6**.17
3:23	**16**.51
3:27	**17**.225
4	**7**.154
4:1–8	**3**.339
4:1–3	**4**.239; **13**.13
4:16	**17**.7
5:1–4	**3**.339; **4**.239; **7**.154; **13**.13
7:2	**17**.19
7:19	**8**.25
8:3–18	**9**.221

8:3	**17**.143
8:18	**6**.48
9:1–7	**17**.23
9:6	**2**.242; **14**.261
10:2	**17**.41
10:8	**14**.263
10:20, 22	**16**.158
11:24	**17**.143
13:3	**14**.312
13:16	**14**.314
14:14, 20	**8**.145
14:21	**17**.9
14:22	**8**.145
15	**6**.172
16	**17**.172
16:15	**17**.142
16:37–39	**16**.143
16:46, 49, 53, 55	**15**.185
17:22ff	**3**.110
17:23	**4**.179
18:4	**8**.26; **10**.82
18:18	**6**.17
18:23	**14**.343
18:31	**5**.131
19:10	**6**.172
20:34	**9**.223
20:37	**6**.56
20:43	**14**.173
21:2	**13**.23
22:27	**1**.281
23:26–29	**16**.143
24:6	**17**.167
26–27	**17**.158
26:3–7	**2**.12
26:13	**17**.166
26:16	**16**.46
27:3	**17**.154
27:28–30	**17**.164

---

1 Matt, v.1	**3** Mark	**5** John, v.1	**7** Acts	**9** Cor
2 Matt, v.2	**4** Luke	**6** John, v.2	**8** Rom	**10** Gal, Eph

28:12–22	2.12	43:3	16.51
28:17	16.151	43:16	17.212
30:2	13.23	44:7, 9	11.139
31:1ff	3.110	44:13	14.106
31:6	2.76; 4.179	45:2	17.212
32:7–8	3.319	47:1–12	5.154, 251
32:7	17.14	47:1–7	17.220
33:12	1.56	47:12	17.221
34	6.54	48:20	17.212
34:9–10	15.194	48:30–35	17.210
34:23ff	3.298	48:31–35	17.201
34:23	14.215; 16.2; 17.38	48:35	16.135
34:24	16.25		
36:25	5.79		
36:26–27	1.48; 5.84, 131	*Daniel*	
37:9	6.274		
37:14	1.48	2:34f, 44f	2.265; 8.135
37:24	3.298; 14.215; 16.2; 17.38	2:44	17.187
		3	9.119; 13.129
37:25	6.128; 16.25	3:19–28	13.164
37:27	9.223; 17.203	3:19–25	1.117
38–39	17.194	3:24–25	8.166
38	17.60	4:10, 21	3.110
38:8	17.133	5:29	16.144
38:14–39	16.8	6:17	17.23
38:19	17.13	6:18, 23	13.164
38:21	17.133	7:1–14	5.185f; 16.36
38:22	17.134	7:1–8	6.121
39:2, 4	17.133	7:3–7	17.88
39:15	1.314	7:8	17.94
39:17–19	17.184	7:9	16.48f
39:17	17.133	7:10	17.196
39:29	1.48	7:13–14	17.115
40:2	17.209	7:13	2.355; 5.185; 6.121; 16.45
40:3	17.67, 211		
40:6	17.67	7:14	6.128; 17.187, 217
41:21	17.212	7:20	17.94
43:1–2	17.151	7:27	16.9; 17.187
43:2	16.48, 50	8:9–12	17.60, 62

8:10	**17.**77	6:6	**1.**335; **2.**24; **3.**296;
8:26	**17.**225		13.115
9:11	**14.**35; **16.**25	8:13	**5.**112
9:27	**3.**309	9:1	**14.**102; **16.**108; **17.**106
10:5	**16.**46	9:3	**5.**59
10:6	**16.**49f; 103	10:1	**6.**172
10:13, 20f	**16.**54	10:8	**17.**16
11	**17.**194	11:1	**1.**35f; **3.**71; **8.**124
11:31	**3.**309; **15.**62	11:8	**15.**185
12:1	**16.**54, 123	11:10	**17.**54
12:2–3	**16.**9	12:5	**16.**39
12:3	**14.**134; **16.**111	13:5	**8.**114
12:7	**17.**69	13:15	**17.**20
12:10	**17.**225	14:6	**8.**149
12:11	**2.**306; **3.**309; **15.**62		

Hosea

1:5	**17.**4
1:6, 9	**14.**197
1:10	**8.**121, 133; **14.**197; **16.**48; **17.**22
1:11	**16.**10
2:1	**14.**197
2:3	**16.**143
2:4	**6.**28
2:8	**17.**6
2:9	**16.**143
2:12	**2.**251
2:18	**3.**24; **16.**10
2:19–20	**16.**76; **17.**172
2:22	**17.**6
2:23	**8.**133; **14.**197
4:6	**6.**208
4:17	**8.**29; **16.**145
5:6	**5.**112
5:8	**11.**58

Joel

1:7–18	**17.**49
2–3	**3.**304
2:1–11	**17.**49
2:1–2	**4.**257; **6.**197; **7.**25; **14.**344; **16.**7
2:1	**17.**16, 42
2:10	**3.**319; **17.**13, 44
2:11	**17.**16
2:23	**14.**121
2:28	**1.**48
2:30–31	**2.**303; **4.**257; **11.**204; **14.**344; **16.**7
2:30	**14.**341
2:31	**17.**14
2:32	**8.**121, 140
3:2, 12	**17.**116
3:13	**17.**115
3:15	**3.**319; **16.**7
3:16	**17.**54
3:18	**5.**251; **17.**220

1 Matt, v.1	**3** Mark	**5** John, v.1	**7** Acts	**9** Cor
2 Matt, v.2	**4** Luke	**6** John, v.2	**8** Rom	**10** Gal, Eph

Amos

1:14	**17**.20
3:2	**8**.114; **11**.11
3:7	**2**.5; **3**.281; **6**.51;
	8.12; **11**.10; **12**.49,
	227; **13**.12; **14**.36;
	14.293; **15**.170;
	16.25, 168
3:8	**17**.54
3:10	**14**.116
3:12	**6**.60
4:11	**15**.185
5:4	**6**.208
5:11	**14**.117
5:16–20	**3**.304
5:18–20	**4**.257; **7**.25
5:18	**11**.204
5:27	**7**.60
7:7–9	**17**.67
7:14–15	**3**.28
8:3	**14**.115
8:4–7	**14**.117
8:8	**17**.13
8:9	**3**.319; **17**.14
9:3	**17**.47
9:5	**16**.39
9:8–10	**8**.145
9:11	**16**.2
9:13	**5**.168
9:14	**12**.79

Micah

1:1–4	**17**.16
1:8–11	**16**.143
2:12	**8**.145
3:3	**17**.148
3:8	**5**.83
3:11	**14**.315
4:1	**15**.59
4:4	**2**.251; **5**.93
4:6	**13**.182
5:2–4	**16**.2
5:2	**1**.24, 30
5:3	**8**.145
6:6–8	**8**.58; **13**.115; **14**.61
6:8	**3**.294
7:6	**3**.313
7:8	**6**.13
7:12	**3**.319
7:18	**1**.56

Nahum

1:3	**17**.19
1:4	**17**.20
1:5–6	**14**.341
1:5	**17**.15
3:4	**17**.142
3:5	**16**.143
3:14	**17**.167

Habakkuk

2:3	**13**.127
2:4	**3**.294; **10**.26
2:14	**6**.208
2:20	**17**.36

Jonah

3:10	**1**.54

Zephaniah

1:3	**17.44**
1:7	**7.25**
1:12	**9.45**
1:14–18	**2.303; 4.257; 14.344**
1:14–16	**11.204**
1:14	**16.7; 17.16**
1:16	**17.42**
2:9	**15.185**
2:11	**5.158**
2:13–15	**17.150**
3:3	**1.281**
3:8	**8.25**
3:9	**17.217**
3:12–13	**8.145**
3:13	**17.108**

Haggai

2:6	**13.188; 17.13**
2:7–9	**16.9**
2:9	**17.201**

Zechariah

1:5	**6.33**
1:6	**3.281; 14.36**
1:18	**16.171**
2:1	**17.67**
2:5	**17.210**
2:12	**5.59**
2:13	**17.217**
3:1–5	**17.30**
3:1–2	**17.81**
3:2	**3.22**
3:10	**2.251**

4:2	**16.45**
4:10	**16.172**
5:3	**1.370**
6:1–8	**16.2**
6:1–5	**17.19**
7:6–10	**14.61**
8:2	**14.104**
8:20–23	**17.217**
8:22–23	**16.130**
9:9	**2.240; 3.264; 4.240; 6.117f**
9:14	**17.20, 42**
10:6–11	**3.319**
10:11	**17.128**
11:10	**2.337**
11:16	**6.62**
12:6	**14.85**
12:10	**6.261; 16.36f**
12:11	**17.132**
13:1	**5.79, 154**
13:4	**1.282**
13:7	**2.343**
14	**17.60**
14:1–11	**16.8; 17.194**
14:1–4	**17.116**
14:8	**5.154; 17.220**
14:9	**17.217**
14:13	**16.7; 17.5**
14:16–18	**5.248**

Malachi

1:2–3	**8.128**
1:8–9	**14.63**
1:11	**5.158**
2:7	**16.54**
2:9	**14.63**

2:10	6.27	3:5	14.119
2:16	1.151; 11.196	4:1	11.204; 14.341
2:17	14.338	4:4	14.35, 293
3:1–4	5.108	4:5–6	1.44; 2.6, 136, 164;
3:1–3	16.7; 17.16		3.213; 4.19, 90;
3:1	1.69; 2.242; 3.12;		5.78; 16.6
	17.70	4:5	17.70

INDEX OF NEW TESTAMENT REFERENCES

(Page numbers in italics indicate the main treatment of the N.T. passages)

5:12	1.179; 17.172	6:5–8	1.191–198
5:13–16	2.54	6:5	1.186
5:13	1.85, 118–122	6:9–15	1.198–200
5:14–15	1.122–125	6:9	1.200–210
5:14	16.53	6:10–11	1.364
5:15	1.85; 3.98	6:10	1.210–214, 258, 267;
5:16	1.125f; 14.72, 204		2.86, 289; 3.42;
5:17–20	1.6, 126–133; 2.282,		4.54f; 14.347
	285	6:11	1.215–219
5:18	1.85	6:12	1.103, 219–224; 3.276;
5:21–48	1.133–137		14.228
5:21–22	1.137–141; 15.83	6:13	1.224–232; 9.196;
5:21	1.9, 134		17.82
5:22	1.140; 3.231	6:14–15	1.103, 219–224; 2.195;
5:23–24	1.142f; 12.65		3.276; 14.22, 71, 228
5:25–26	1.144–146	6:14	14.134
5:26	4.171	6:15	12.65
5:27–28	1.146	6:16–18	1.232–238, 335
5:27	1.9, 134	6:16	1.186
5:28	14.331	6:19–21	1.238–243
5:29–30	1.147–150; 11.150	6:19	14.116
5:29	1.140; 3.231	6:21	2.218
5:30	1.140; 2.183; 3.231	6:22–23	1.243–247
5:31–32	1.85, 150–157; 4.212	6:24	1.248–254; 14.103;
5:31	3.237		15.57; 16.109
5:33–37	1.158–162; 2.292;	6:25–34	1.254–261; 14.272
	14.126	6:26–30	2.54
5:33	1.134	7:1–5	1.85, 261–265
5:34–37	14.22	7:1–2	2.89; 6.6; 14.66, 71,
5:34	1.9		121
5:38–42	1.162–172	7:2	3.98; 17.153
5:38	1.9, 134	7:3–5	6.6
5:43–48	1.172–178	7:6	1.265–269; 3.178;
5:43	1.9, 134		11.54
5:47	9.163	7:7–12	1.85
6:1–18	1.179–185	7:7–11	1.85, 270–272
6:1	1.185f	7:7	4.8; 5.246
6:2–4	1.187–191	7:11	3.27
6:2	1.186	7:12	1.272–277

	12.170; **15**.68; **16**.123	12:30	**2**.*39–41*
10:33	**15**.119	12:31–33	**2**.*41–45*
10:34–39	**1**.*393–397*	12:31–32	**4**.161
10:34	**6**.185	12:34–37	**2**.*45–47*
10:36	**1**.228; **3**.75; **4**.103	12:36–37	**14**.82
10:37–39	**2**.151	12:38–42	**2**.*48–50*
10:39	**6**.124; **17**.84	12:38–40	**2**.129
10:40–42	**1**.*397–400*	12:39	**16**.108
10:42	**1**.179	12:43–45	**2**.20, *50–52*
11	**11**.1	12:45	**14**.335
11:1–6	**2**.*1–4*; **5**.245; **6**.163	12:46–50	**2**.20, *52f*; **14**.9
11:4	**5**.196	13	**1**.8; **2**.*53–56*
11:5	**14**.66	13:1–9	**2**.*56–63*; **14**.57, 189
11:7–11	**2**.*4–7*	13:8	**6**.154
11:12–15	**2**.*7–9*	13:10–17	**2**.*63–71*
11:16–19	**2**.*9–10*	13:12	**3**.98
11:16–17	**2**.54	13:13	**4**.99
11:20–24	**2**.*11–13*	13:14–15	**6**.132
11:23–24	**1**.371	13:18–23	**2**.*56–63*
11:24	**15**.185	13:19	**15**.24
11:25–27	**2**.*13–15*	13:24–30	**2**.*71–75*; **12**.179;
11:27	**15**.67		**17**.115
11:28–30	**2**.*15–18*	13:31–32	**2**.*75–78*; **4**.179
11:29	**10**.51	13:33	**2**.*78–83*
11:30	**10**.51; **11**.157; **15**.104	13:34–35	**1**.6; **2**.63–71
12	**2**.*18–20*	13:36–43	**2**.*71–75*; **12**.179
12:1–8	**2**.19, *21–27*, 42	13:37–43	**17**.115
12:7	**1**.335	13:39	**17**.82
12:9–14	**2**.19, *27–32*	13:43	**16**.122
12:10–13	**4**.72	13:44	**2**.*83–86*
12:14	**1**.7; **2**.19	13:45–46	**2**.*86–88*
12:15–21	**2**.*32–34*	13:46	**17**.215
12:15	**1**.2	13:47–50	**2**.*88–90*; **12**.179
12:16	**1**.298	13:51–52	**2**.*90f*
12:22–29	**2**.19, *34–39*	13:53–58	**2**.*91f*
12:23	**1**.15; **3**.298	13:55	**3**.6; **4**.13; **14**.9, 14,
12:24	**1**.7		19; **15**.170
12:25–29	**15**.78	13:57	**5**.172
12:28	**12**.90	13:58	**1**.3

26:42	**15.**115
26:45	**5.**102
26:47–50	**2.***334–336*
26:50–56	**2.***350–352*
26:52	**17.**97
26:53	**6.**67; **17.**182
26:56	**14.**154, 268
26:57–58	**2.***344–347*
26:57	**2.***352–356*; **14.**263
26:59–68	**2.***352–356*
26:61	**5.**115
26:63	**1.**161; **6.**245
26:64	**16.**36
26:65–66	**2.**357; **6.**235
26:69–75	**2.***344–347*; **14.**90
27:1–2	**2.**353, *356–362*
27:1	**14.**263
27:3–10	**2.***336–338*
27:3–5	**3.**330; **7.**16
27:3	**14.**263
27:9	**1.**6
27:11–26	**2.**353, *356–362*
27:11	**1.**9
27:14	**6.**245
27:15–26	**6.**248
27:17, 22	**2.**361
27:27–31	**2.***362–364*
27:32–44	**2.***365–367*
27:34	**4.**284
27:35	**1.**6; **14.**267
27:37	**1.**9
27:45–50	**2.***367–370*
27:50	**2.**369; **3.**364; **4.**288; **6.**258
27:51–56	**2.***370f*
27:54	**1.**301; **6.**193, 205
27:56	**5.**16; **6.**256; **14.**8, 16
27:57–61	**2.***371–374*
27:57	**2.**219

27:62–66	**2.***374*
27:66	**6.**266; **16.**166; **17.**23, 191
28:1–10	**2.***375f*
28:2	**4.**291
28:3	**17.**121
28:9	**6.**270
28:10	**6.**271
28:11–15	**2.**377
28:16–20	**2.***377f*
28:18	**1.**9
28:19–20	**1.**6, 363; **6.**64
28:20	**6.**192; **7.**10; **17.**232

Mark

1:1–4	**3.***11–15*
1:3	**4.**6; **5.**78f
1:5–8	**3.***15–18*
1:8	**15.**108
1:9–11	**3.***18–21*; **15.**108
1:11	**6.**127
1:12–13	**3.***21–24*
1:12	**1.**64; **3.**6
1:13	**17.**82
1:14–15	**3.***24–26*
1:14	**1.**210; **5.**2, 141; **7.**11
1:15	**1.**51; **4.**54
1:16–20	**3.***26–29*
1:19–20	**5.**16; **10.**149; **14.**9
1:19	**14.**273
1:20	**3.**254; **4.**16; **6.**229
1:21–28	**1.**308
1:21–22	**3.***29–32*
1:21	**4.**187
1:22	**1.**133; **3.**6
1:23–28	**3.***33–36*

9:4	**17.**71	10:32	**3.**7
9:5	**5.**4	10:35–45	**2.**228
9:7	**6.**127	10:35–40	**3.***253–256*
9:9–13	**3.***212–214*	10:35	**1.**3; **5.**16; **14.**9
9:14–18	**3.***214–216*	10:37	**17.**148
9:14	**5.**9	10:41–45	**3.***256–259*
9:19–24	**3.***216–218*	10:41	**14.**9, 190
9:22	**1.**354	10:42–44	**14.**267
9:25–29	**3.***218–220*	10:45	**14.**317; **16.**177
9:30–31	**3.***220f*	10:46–52	**3.***259–262*
9:31	**3.**252	10:47ff	**1.**349; **3.**298
9:32–35	**3.***221–224*	11:1–6	**3.***262–265*
9:36–37	**3.***224f*	11:1–2	**3.**8
9:38–40	**3.***225–228*	11:1	**2.**238
9:38	**5.**16	11:7–10	**3.***266–268*
9:40	**2.**40	11:9	**11.**2
9:41–42	**3.***228–230*	11:11	**3.***268f*; **16.**49
9:43–48	**3.***230–233*	11:12–14	**2.**251; **3.***269–272*
9:43	**1.**141	11:12	**3.**7
9:44–48	**1.**141	11:13	**2.**252
9:45	**1.**141	11:15–19	**3.***272–275*
9:47	**1.**141	11:15–17	**5.**4, 107
9:49–50	**3.***233–236*	11:17	**5.**111, 113
10:1–12	**3.***236–240*	11:20–21	**2.**251; **3.***269–272*
10:9	**9.**62	11:22–26	**3.***275–278*
10:11–12	**2.**201	11:27–33	**3.***278–280*
10:13–16	**3.**7, *241f*	12:1–12	**3.***280–284*
10:14	**1.**3; **3.**7	12:9	**14.**166
10:17–22	**2.**213; **3.***243–245*	12:10	**14.**194
10:18	**2.**213	12:13–17	**3.***284–288*
10:21	**3.**7; **5.**19; **6.**145; **16.**49; **17.**107	12:14	**14.**62
10:23–27	**3.***246–248*	12:18–27	**3.***288–292*
10:23	**16.**49	12:28–34	**2.**278; **3.***292–297*
10:24	**3.**6	12:28–31	**15.**102
10:25	**7.**2	12:35–37a	**1.**349; **3.***297–299*
10:26	**3.**6	12:37b–40	**3.***299–301*
10:28–31	**3.***248–250*	12:41–44	**3.***301–303*
10:32–34	**2.**227; **3.***251–253*	12:42	**4.**171
		13	**3.***303*

11 Phil, Col, Thes
12 Tim, Tit, Phlm
13 Heb
14 Jas, Pet
15 John, Jude
16 Rev, v.1
17 Rev, v.2

1:5–25	4.8–11	3:23	1.41; 3.139; 4.37, 41;
1:5	5.76		14.19
1:26–38	4.11–13	3:38	4.3
1:36	2.96; 5.82	4:1–13	4.41–44
1:39–45	4.13f	4:1	3.6
1:46–56	4.4, 14–16	4:2–3, 5	17.82
1:46–47	12.18	4:6–7	16.33
1:47	15.207	4:13	2.148; 17.82
1:55	15.78	4:14–15	4.44–46
1:57–66	4.16–18	4:16–30	4.46–49
1:67–80	4.4, 18f	4:16	16.26
1:80	17.143	4:18	14.66
2:1–7	4.20f	4:24	5.172
2:7	14.20	4:25–27	4.5
2:8–20	4.22f	4:25	14.132
2:21–24	4.23–25	4:31–37	4.49–51
2:24	4.5	4:35	7.2
2:25–35	4.25–27	4:38–39	4.51–53
2:29–32	4.4	4:38	4.187
2:36–40	4.27f	4:40–44	4.53–55
2:36	16.105	4:40	1.2
2:41–52	4.28f	4:43	1.210; 4.120
2:48	4.12	5:1–11	4.55–57
2:49	2.169; 4.120	5:7–10	5.16
3:1–6	4.30–32	5:8	3.80; 5.163; 10.102
3:1–2	4.3; 7.93	5:10	14.9
3:3–11	7.141	5:11	16.51
3:4, 6	4.6; 5.79	5:12–15	4.57–59
3:7–18	4.32–35	5:16–17	4.59–61
3:7–13	3.20	5:16	4.4
3:8	3.271; 6.26; 14.72	5:17–26	1.1; 3.2
3:16	5.85; 7.141; 15.109	5:18–26	4.61–63
3:18	5.2	5:27–32	1.333; 4.63–65, 234
3:19–20	4.35f	5:33–35	4.65–67
3:19	7.93	5:36–39	4.67–69
3:20	5.2	6:1–5	4.69–71
3:21–22	4.37f; 15.108	6:6–11	4.71–73
3:21	4.4	6:6	4.187
3:23–38	3.298; 4.12, 38–41	6:7	2.19

1:26	5.195	3:7–13	*5.130–133*
1:28	5.6	3:11	16.32, 140
1:29–31	*5.80–82*	3:14–15	*5.134–137*
1:29	5.195; 15.77; 16.170	3:16	5.13, 43, *137–138*;
1:32, 34	*5.82–85*; 15.108, 112		6.18; 12.19, 55;
1:35–39	5.75, *85–88*		15.40; 17.205
1:35–36	1.78; 5.195	3:17–21	*5.138–140*
1:36	16.170	3:17	6.18
1:40–42	5.75, *88–91*; 8.221	3:19–20	5.46, 47
1:40–41	5.5	3:19	15.27
1:41–51	5.76	3:21	5.68; 14.133; 15.29
1:41–42	14.292	3:22–30	5.2, *141–144*
1:43–51	5.76, *91–95*	3:25–30	5.50
1:43	17.107	3:28	5.12
1:44	5.6, 202	3:29	17.173
1:45	5.52	3:31–36	*5.144–146*
1:48	2.252; 6.82	3:36	5.44
1:51	16.140, 150	4	5.5
2:1–13	5.2	4:1–9	*5.146–151*
2:1–12	5.106, 232	4:1–4	5.172, 228
2:1–11	5.5, 76, *95–105*	4:1	5.50
2:1	5.6; 14.19	4:1–2	5.2, 12, 228
2:4	5.15, 231	4:4–42	1.363
2:6	5.5	4:5	5.6
2:11	5.9, 68, 75	4:6	5.14
2:12–16	*5.105–114*	4:9	4.5, 129; 5.6; 7.65
2:13–22	5.4	4:10–15a	*5.151–156*; 6.86
2:13–17	10.156	4:14	5.250; 17.37
2:13	3.263; 5.2, 4, 80	4:15b–21	*5.156–158*
2:15	5.14	4:16–17	5.15
2:16	5.111	4:21	5.116
2:17–22	*5.114–117*	4:22–26	*5.158–162*
2:20	5.6	4:26	6.72
2:23–25	*5.117–120*	4:27–30	*5.162–164*
2:23	5.228	4:29	9.132
3:1–15	5.5; 14.171	4:31–34	*5.164–166*
3:1–6	*5.120–130*	4:31	5.14
3:3–8	6.86	4:35–5:1	5.2
3:3, 5	16.140	4:35–38	*5.166–169*

11 Phil, Col, Thes
12 Tim, Tit, Phlm
13 Heb
14 Jas, Pet
15 John, Jude
16 Rev, v.1
17 Rev, v.2

7:1–9	5.*230–233*; **6**.83	8:25	**6**.19
7:1–5	**14**.19	8:28	**5**.135; **16**.23
7:1	**5**.176	8:29	**5**.166
7:2	**5**.2, 106; **6**.10	8:31–32	**5**.67; *6.20–22*
7:3–9	**14**.9	8:33–36	*6.22–24*
7:5	**2**.52; **6**.257; **7**.96;	8:33	**15**.78
	9.144; **14**.9	8:37–41	*6.24–26*
7:6, 8	**5**.102	8:37	**15**.78
7:10–13	*5.233–238*	8:39	**6**.64
7:10	**3**.263; **5**.2, 15, 106	8:40	**5**.67; **9**.146
7:14	*5.242–245*	8:41–45	*6.27–29*
7:15–24	**5**.239	8:44	**9**.147
7:15–18	*5.238–240*	8:45	**5**.68
7:16	**16**.23	8:46–50	*6.29–32*
7:17	**12**.171	8:48	**4**.140
7:18	**5**.69	8:50	**5**.69
7:19–24	*5.241–242*	8:51–55	*6.32–33*
7:21–23	**5**.6	8:54	**5**.69
7:25–30	*5.242–245*	8:56–59	*6.34–36*
7:30	**5**.231	8:58	**5**.14
7:31–36	*5.245–247*	9	**5**.10; **6**.50–52
7:33	**6**.156	9:1–5	*6.37–41*
7:37–44	*5.247–252*	9:3	**5**.9
7:37	**6**.10; **17**.37	9:4	**4**.168
7:38–39	**17**.221	9:5	**1**.122; **5**.45; **13**.56
7:39	**6**.81	9:6–12	*6.41–44*
7:45–52	*5.253–254*	9:6	**5**.6
7:53–8:11	*6.1–9*	9:13–16	*6.44–45*
8:2–11	**6**.292f	9:14	**4**.187; **5**.6
8:12–20	*6.9–15*	9:17–35	*6.46–49*
8:12	**5**.45, 48; **6**.64; **15**.27;	9:25	**5**.53
	17.229	9:35–41	*6.49–50*
8:14	**5**.51	9:35–38	**15**.68
8:15	**6**.292	9:37	**6**.72
8:16	**5**.9	9:38	**5**.53
8:18	**5**.51; **15**.112	9:39	**5**.139
8:20	**5**.231	9:41	**7**.35
8:21–30	*6.15–20*	10:1–18	**14**.215, 270
8:23	**6**.18	10:1–6	*6.52–57*

1 Matt, v.1	**3** Mark	**5** John, v.1	**7** Acts	**9** Cor
2 Matt, v.2	**4** Luke	**6** John, v.2	**8** Rom	**10** Gal, Eph

13:1–17	5.5; 6.*136–142*	14:25–31	6.*170–171*
13:1	6.292	14:30	9.196; 17.82
13:2	17.82	15:1–10	6.*172–176*
13:4–5	14.270	15:1	5.9
13:18–20	6.*142–144*	15:7	15.115
13:21–30	6.*144–147*	15:10	6.75
13:23–25	5.19	15:11–17	6.*176–181*
13:27	3.330; 17.82	15:14	2.53
13:29	6.293	15:16	8.12; 11.103
13:30	3.348; 5.48; 6.85	15:18–21	6.*181–186*
13:31, 32	6.*147–149*	15:18–19	6.18; 14.87
13:33–35	6.*149–150*	15:19	15.4
13:34–35	14.227; 15.88, 141	15:22–25	6.*186–187*
13:34	6.75; 15.44	15:22	7.35
13:36–38	6.*151–152*	15:24	5.52
14–17	5.5	15:26, 27	6.*187–188*
14:1–3	6.*152–156*	15:26	5.53, 67; 15.112
14:4–6	6.*156–159*	15:27	5.53
14:5	5.5	16:1–4	6.*189–191*
14:6–9	15.67	16:2	6.47; 17.10
14:6	5.43, 66f	16:5–11	6.*191–194*
14:7–11	6.*159–163*	16:11	9.44, 196; 17.82
14:8–9	5.5	16:12–15	6.*194–196*
14:9	1.21; 2.15; 4.137, 288; 6.210; 9.197; 13.103; 14.197; 16.22	16:12–13	5.24
		16:13–14	14.133
		16:13	5.67
		16:16–24	6.*196–200*
14:10	5.239	16:22	1.89; 11.51; 16.97
14:11	5.52	16:25–28	6.*200–201*
14:12–14	6.*163–165*	16:29–33	6.*201–203*
14:14	15.115	16:33	6.18; 16.178
14:15–17	6.*166–168*	17:1–5	6.*204–209*
14:15	6.75; 15.141	17:1	5.102
14:17	5.67; 6.18; 14.87	17:2	5.43
14:18–24	6.*168–169*	17:4	4.167; 5.166
14:19	4.88; 16.53	17:5	5.14, 69
14:21	5.128; 6.75	17:6–8	6.*209–213*
14:22	14.87; 15.169	17:9–19	6.*213–217*
14:23–24	5.166; 6.75	17:11	6.75

17:14	**15.**4
17:15	1.287
17:20, 21	6.75, *217–218*
17:21–23	14.224
17:22–26	6.*219–220*
17:22	**5.**69
17:25	**6.**18
18:1–11	6.*220–224*
18:1	**5.**6
18:10	2.351; 3.346; 5.220
18:13	4.32, 242
18:12–14	6.*225–227*
18:15–18	6.*227–231*
18:15	4.270
18:19–24	6.*225–227*
18:25–27	6.*227–231*
18:28– 19:16	6.*231–249*
18:28	6.293
18:33–34	2.138
18:36	**14.**87
18:37	5.67; **12.**200; **14.**133; **16.**32
18:40	3.173
19:6–7	4.280
19:10–11	**6.**67
19:11	**5.**15
19:12	4.281
19:13	**5.**6
19:14	6.293
19:17–22	6.*249–252*
19:17	4.282; **5.**6
19:23, 24	2.367; 4.285; 6.*253– 255*
19:23	3.142; **5.**5
19:25–27	**5.**19; 6.*255–257*
19:25	**14.**8, 16, 17
19:26–27	**14.**154; **15.**138
19:26	5.98; **14.**18
19:28–30	6.*257–259*
19:28	**5.**14
19:30	2.369; 3.364; 4.288
19:31–37	6.*260–262*
19:34	**5.**251
19:35	**5.**19, 53
19:38–42	6.*262–264*
19:39	2.219; **5.**5, 121
20:1–10	6.*264–268*
20:1	**5.**48
20:2	**5.**19
20:11–18	6.*268–272*
20:12	4.291
20:19–23	6.*272–274*
20:20	6.282
20:24–29	**5.**5; 6.*275–279*
20:27	6.270
20:28	**14.**294
20:29	**14.**161, 179
20:30, 31	6.*279*
20:31	**5.**43
21	6.280
21:1–14	6.*280–284*
21:1	2.105; **5.**208
21:2	**5.**6, 94
21:6	**5.**220
21:11	**5.**220; 6.284
21:15–19	6.54, *284–287*; **14.**269
21:16	**10.**148; **14.**215
21:18–19	**14.**287, 308
21:19–22	**17.**108
21:20–24	6.*287–288*
21:20	**5.**19
21:24	**5.**19, 53
21:25	2.11; 4.134; 6.*288–289*

Acts

1:1–6:7	7.5

5:12–16	7.45–46	8:25	7.77; 15.24
5:17–32	7.46–48	8:26–40	7.6, 67–69
5:17	14.316	8:29	7.19
5:29	14.206	9:1–9	6.193; 7.69–71
5:30–31	14.141	9:2	7.139; 9.186
5:30	7.27	9:4	17.85
5:31	5.135; 13.25; 14.141	9:9	9.258
5:32	7.20	9:10–18	7.71–72; 12.44
5:33–42	7.48–50	9:11	15.169
6:1–7	7.50–52	9:13	11.11
6:1	12.106	9:19–22	7.72–73
6:2	15.24	9:23–25	7.74–75; 9.255
6:3	7.19	9:25	3.184
6:5	16.67	9:26–31	7.75–76
6:7	15.24	9:26–28	12.44
6:8–9:31	7.5	9:27, 30	7.90
6:8–15	7.52–53	9:31–	7.6
6:12	14.263	10:48	
6:14	5.115	9:32–	7.5
6:15	14.259	12:24	
7:1–7	7.53–55	9:32–43	7.76–78
7:6	14.201	9:32	11.11
7:8–16	7.55–57	9:43	7.80
7:17–36	7.57–59	10	2.145; 11.145; 14.292
7:37–53	7.59–61	10:1–8	7.78–80
7:51	7.19	10:6	14.254
7:52	14.120	10:9–16	7.80–81
7:53	10.29; 13.17; 16.24	10:17–33	7.81–83
7:54–8:1	7.61–63	10:17	1.301
7:55	7.19	10:19	7.19
7:60	4.285; 6.86; 8.168	10:22–23	1.300; 4.84
8:1–4	7.63–64	10:26	1.301
8:5–13	7.64–65	10:28	4.85
8:9, 11	1.26	10:34–43	7.83–84; 14.140
8:14–25	7.65–67	10:34	14.62, 141
8:14–17	10.23	10:36–43	9.17
8:14	5.16	10:38	15.70, 108; 17.82
8:17–18	15.89	10:39–42	14.141
8:17	13.55; 15.70, 109	10:39	14.178

10:42, 43	**14**.141	13:5	**11**.170; **12**.217; **15**.24
10:44–48	*7.84–85*	13:6–12	**9**.21
10:44–46	**7**.66	13:6	**1**.26
10:44–45	**15**.90	13:7	**15**.24
10:44	**10**.23; **15**.109	13:8	**1**.26
10:46	**7**.21	13:9	**7**.19
11:1–10	*7.85–86*	13:11	**12**.54
11:1	**15**.24	13:12	**7**.3
11:11–18	*7.86–87*	13:13	**3**.3; *7.100–102*;
11:12	**7**.19		**10**.39; **11**.170;
11:19–30	**7**.6		**12**.217; **14**.275
11:19–21	*7.87–89*	13:14–15	*7.102–103*
11:20	**8**.215f	13:15	**16**.26
11:22–26	*7.89–90*	13:16–41	*7.103–105*
11:24	**7**.19	13:26	**15**.24
11:27–30	*7.91–92*, 97	13:27	**4**.285
11:28	**7**.19	13:29	**7**.26
11:30	**14**.264	13:35	**5**.117; **13**.83; **15**.24
12:1–11	*7.92–94*	13:38	**15**.53
12:2	**2**.230; **3**.256; **7**.1, 101;	13:42–52	*7.105–107*
	14.15	13:44, 49	**15**.24
12:12–19	*7.94–96*	13:50	**12**.197; **14**.149; **16**.79
12:12	**3**.3, 347; **12**.217	14:1–7	*7.107–108*
12:15	**16**.54	14:2	**16**.79
12:17	**14**.10	14:3	**15**.24
12:20–25	*7.96–97*	14:4	**10**.145
12:24	**15**.24	14:5–6	**12**.197
12:25–	*7.5*	14:5	**16**.79
16:5		14:8–21	**12**.21
12:25–	**7**.6	14:8–18	*7.108–109*
14:8		14:8	**6**.37
12:25	**3**.3	14:14	**10**.145; **14**.17
13–14	**7**.97	14:15	**17**.10
13:1–3	*7.98–99*; **12**.49	14:17	**8**.27
13:1	**3**.361; *7.91*; **8**.219;	14:19, 20	*7.109–110*
	14.79; **17**.127	14:19	**12**.197; **16**.79
13:2	**7**.19, 101; **8**.13	14:21–28	*7.110–112*
13:4–12	*7.99–100*	14:21–23	**15**.137
13:4	**7**.19, 101	14:22	**12**.198; **16**.40

18:5	**11**.47; **12**.22; **14**.143, 275	19:31	**7**.3, 140
		19:33	**8**.216
18:8	**9**.16	19:34	**1**.196
18:9–10	**11**.27, 215	19:37	**7**.4
18:11	**9**.31	20:1–6	**7**.*147–148*
18:12–17	**7**.*136–137*; **14**.146	20:4	**8**.220; **9**.169; **12**.22, 222; **15**.148
18:12	**7**.3		
18:14	**7**.4	20:5–16	**7**.6
18:18–23	**7**.*137–138*	20:5	**16**.28
18:18	**8**.8, 209	20:7–12	**7**.*148–150*
18:19	**16**.60	20:13–16	**7**.*150–151*
18:24–28	**7**.*138–141*	20:17–38	**7**.*151–152*; **16**.60
18:24–26	**8**.209; **13**.9	20:17	**16**.28
18:24	**9**.14; **12**.266; **16**.60	20:28–29	**14**.264; **15**.194
18:26	**11**.68; **13**.9; **16**.60	20:28	**10**.148
19	**9**.253; **16**.59; **17**.93	20:17–35	**10**.63
19:1–7	**5**.11; **7**.*141–142*	20:17	**12**.71
19:3–4	**5**.50	20:23	**7**.19
19:6	**7**.21; **13**.55	20:28	**6**.54; **7**.19; **12**.71; **14**.161
19:8–12	**7**.*142–143*		
19:9	**7**.139	20:29–31	**16**.119
19:10	**8**.20; **11**.94	20:29–30	**15**.4, 64; **16**.63
19:13–41	**16**.15	20:29	**1**.281; **6**.61
19:13–20	**7**.*143–144*	20:31	**9**.31; **10**.63; **16**.60
19:13	**1**.289	20:32	**15**.24
19:19	**17**.206	20:33	**14**.116, 266
19:21– 28:31	**7**.5	21–22	**17**.93
		21:1–18	**7**.6
19:21–41	**14**.203	21:1–16	**7**.*153–154*
19:21ff	**15**.153	21:9–10	**7**.91; **12**.68
19:21, 22	**7**.*144*; **8**.2; **11**.47; **12**.22	21:9	**16**.105
		21:15–17	**14**.161
19:22	**12**.222	21:16	**14**.254
19:23–41	**7**.*145–147*	21:17–26	**7**.*154–156*
19:23	**7**.139	21:18–25	**14**.11, 14, 264
19:24–27	**1**.378	21:27–36	**7**.*156–157*
19:25	**12**.214	21:28–29	**10**.112
19:28	**12**.89	21:29	**12**.222
19:29	**11**.169; **15**.147	21:30–40	**16**.15

8–10	**9.**71; **16.**106	11:32	**16.**145
8	**9.**73, *74–76*	12	**9.**95; **14.**255
8:6	**5.**41; **11.**100	12:1–3	**9.***106–107*
9	**9.**73	12:3	**15.**90
9:1–14	**9.***77–81*	12:4–11	**9.**12, *108–112*
9:1	**10.**146	12:9	**6.**164
9:5	**2.**175; **14.**145, 277; **15.**171	12:10	**15.**90
		12:12–31	**9.***112–116*; **14.**225
9:6–7	**12.**161; **14.**17	12:12–27	**8.**159
9:12	**14.**266	12:12	**6.**273
9:15–23	**9.***81–84*	12:13	**12.**272
9:16	**14.**265	12:26	**14.**226
9:22	**16.**93	12:28	**6.**164; **14.**79; **17.**127
9:24–27	**9.***84–86*; **12.**161	12:30	**6.**164
9:24	**11.**45	13	**9.**95, *116–119*; **12.**201
9:25	**10.**52; **16.**83	13:4–7	**9.***119–125*
9:26–27	**11.**45	13:8–13	**9.***125–126*
10:1–13	**9.**73, *87–90*	13:11	**10.**34
10:4	**5.**251	13:12	**6.**220; **14.**179
10:5–11	**15.**182	14	**7.**21; **15.**90
10:11	**14.**250	14:1–23	**9.**96
10:14–22	**9.**73, *91–93*	14:1–19	**9.***126–130*
10:17	**14.**225	14:2	**15.**90
10:23– 11:1	**9.***93–96*	14:6	**16.**22
		14:15	**14.**127
10:23–26, 27–28	**9.**73	14:20–25	**9.***131–133*
		14:20	**13.**50
10:29– 11:1	**9.**74	14:22	**14.**124
		14:23–33	**9.**96
10:31	**14.**214	14:23	**7.**22; **15.**90
11–14	**9.**95	14:24–36	**9.**96
11:2–16	**9.**95, *96–100*	14:26–33	**9.***133–135*
11:10	**14.**322	14:26–27	**15.**90
11:17–22	**9.**95, *100–102*; **15.**192	14:26	**14.**127
11:18–19	**14.**316	14:29	**16.**63
11:21	**15.**194	14:33	**11.**82; **15.**90
11:23–34	**9.***102–105*	14:34–40	**9.***135–137*
11:24–34	**9.**95	14:34	**16.**105
11:30	**15.**118	15	**9.***137–141*; **12.**30

5:22–23	14.301; 17.222
6:1–5	10.52–53
6:1	10.149
6:6–10	10.53–55
6:11–18	10.55–57
6:11	9.258
6:15	5.126
6:16	14.41, 166; 16.130; 17.24
6:17	11.64, 175

Ephesians

1:1–14	10.73–74
1:1–2	10.74–76
1:1	8.xi; 10.63; 11.9
1:2–3	10.129
1:2	8.xi; 11.12; 12.23; 14.36
1:3–14	10.64, 76
1:3–4	10.76–79
1:3	8.xi; 14.153
1:4	14.153; 17.96, 108
1:5–6	10.79–80
1:7–8	10.81–83
1:7	17.31
1:9–10	10.66, 83–85
1:11–14	10.85–88
1:13	3.25; 15.25
1:15–23	10.64, 88–94
1:15	10.63
1:17	10.129, 130; 16.22
1:18	15.177
1:20, 21	14.153
1:21	8.118
1:23	6.273
2:1–10	10.94–95
2:1–9	10.64

2:1–3	10.95–101
2:1	16.116
2:2	9.192; 17.80
2:4–10	10.101–105
2:5	16.116
2:11–12	10.106–110
2:11–13	14.291
2:11	10.62
2:12	14.172
2:13–18	10.110–117
2:13–14	14.225
2:18	6.58; 10.129; 14.235
2:19–22	10.117–119
2:20–21	17.68
2:20	2.141; 3.283; 8.135
3:1–13	10.119–120
3:1–7	10.64, 120–125
3:1	10.61; 11.21, 174
3:2–13	10.119f
3:2	10.63
3:3	16.22
3:6	3.25
3:8–13	10.125–127
3:8	16.179
3:10	8.118
3:12	10.129; 14.235
3:14–21	10.127–128
3:14–17	10.128–132
3:18–21	10.132–133
3:20	15.206
4	10.133–134
4:1–10	10.134–145
4:1–3	10.134–140
4:1	10.61; 11.174; 15.177
4:2	10.52
4:3–6	14.225
4:4–6	10.140–143
4:4	15.177
4:6	10.130; 17.205

Philippians

6:3–5	12.*123–128*
6:4	12.5, 29
6:5	12.6; 14.315
6:6–8	12.*128–131*
6:6	15.198
6:9–10	12.*131–133*; 14.117
6:10	1.252
6:11–16	12.*133–136*
6:11	14.301
6:15	15.163
6:16	16.151
6:17–19	12.*137–138*
6:20–21	12.*138–141*
6:20	12.6, 28

2 Timothy

1:1–7	12.*142–145*
1:2	12.23
1:5	7.120; 11.147; 12.21, 68
1:8–11	12.*145–150*
1:10	3.25; 16.53
1:12–14	12.*150–154*
1:12	4.120; 9.78; 14.296
1:13	15.25
1:14	12.4
1:15–18	12.*154–157*
1:16	12.222
2:1–2	12.*157–158*
2:3–4	12.*159–160*
2:5	11.46; 12.*160–162*
2:6–7	12.*162–163*
2:8–10	12.*163–168*
2:8	1.15; 3.298; 12.4; 15.25
2:11–13	12.*168–170*

2:11–12	6.220
2:12	14.258; 16.40
2:14	12.*170–172*
2:15–18	12.*172–176*
2:15	15.25
2:16	12.29
2:17	12.53
2:18	12.6, 30
2:19	12.*176–178*
2:20–21	12.*178–179*
2:22–26	12.*179–181*
2:23	12.5, 29
2:24	14.293
3:1	12.*182–183*; 14.175
3:2–5	12.*184–191*
3:5	16.118
3:6–7	12.*191–193*
3:6	12.5, 30
3:8–9	12.*193–195*
3:8	12.3; 15.30
3:10–13	12.*195–198*
3:14–17	12.*198–202*
3:15	12.1
4:1–5	12.*202–208*
4:1	14.122; 17.195
4:3	14.80
4:4	12.29
4:5	10.147
4:6–8	12.*308–312*
4:6	17.11
4:8	11.45; 14.49; 16.83
4:9–15	12.*212–220*
4:10	11.171; 14.103; 15.153
4:11	3.4; 7.1f, 101, 192; 11.171
4:14	12.53
4:16–22	12.*220–223*
4:18	8.21

24	3.4; **7**.1; **11**.170, 171; **12**.213, 216; **15**.153

Hebrews

1:1–3	**13**.*12–16*
1:2	**5**.41; **14**.175
1:4–14	**13**.*16–20*
2:1–4	**13**.*20–22*
2:2	**10**.29
2:3	**13**.5, 6
2:4	**16**.32
2:5–9	**13**.*23–25*
2:10–18	**13**.*25–28*
2:18	**4**.271; **9**.171; **16**.132
3:1–6	**13**.*28–32*
3:1	**15**.177
3:7–19	**13**.*32–34*
3:12	**13**.35
3:18–4:2	**15**.182
4:1–10	**13**.*35–38*
4:2	**15**.24
4:11–13	**13**.*38–41*
4:12	**16**.51, 94; **17**.182
4:14–16	**13**.*41–44*
4:14–15	**15**.93
4:14	**6**.154
4:16	**14**.106; **16**.35
5:1–10	**13**.*44–48*, 64
5:1, 3	**14**.233
5:11–14	**13**.*49–51*
5:12–14	**5**.126
5:12	**13**.5–7; **14**.192
5:13	**15**.25
6	**13**.64
6:1–3	**13**.*51–55*
6:2	**14**.192
6:4–8	**13**.*55–59*

6:4–6	**15**.119
6:9–12	**13**.*59–61*
6:10	**13**.6
6:13–20	**13**.*61–63*
6:18	**13**.59
6:20	**6**.155
7	**13**.*63–71*
7:1–3	**13**.69, *71–75*
7:3	**13**.68
7:4–10	**13**.*75–77*
7:8	**13**.70
7:11–20	**13**.*77–79*
7:11	**13**.70
7:15–19	**13**.70
7:19	**14**.106
7:21–25	**13**.*79–83*
7:25	**10**.133; **15**.38
7:26–28	**13**.*83–85*
7:27	**13**.71; **14**.233
8:1–6	**13**.*86–89*
8:5	**17**.10
8:7–13	**13**.*90–94*
9:1–5	**13**.*94–97*
9:4	**16**.94
9:6–10	**13**.*97–101*
9:11–14	**13**.*102–105*
9:14	**17**.31
9:15–22	**13**.*105–108*
9:23–28	**13**.*109–111*
9:23	**17**.10
9:24	**15**.38
9:28	**14**.233
10:1–10	**13**.*112–115*
10:4	**13**.59; **16**.79
10:10	**14**.233
10:11–18	**13**.*116–118*
10:19–25	**13**.*118–123*
10:19–23	**13**.2; **15**.114
10:19–22	**16**.35

James

11 Phil, Col, Thes
12 Tim, Tit, Phlm
13 Heb
14 Jas, Pet
15 John, Jude
16 Rev, v.1
17 Rev, v.2

3:17	**14**.159	5:1	**12**.71; **14**.139, 140,
3:18–22	**6**.35; **14**.*243–245*		141, 154, 161
3:18b–20	**14**.*236–243*	5:2–3	**6**.54; **10**.148; **12**.71
3:18–20	**16**.52	5:2	**14**.161, 215
3:18	**14**.120	5:4	**10**.48; **14**.139, 141,
3:19	**14**.235		160; **16**.83
3:20	**10**.51, 139	5:5	**8**.37; **12**.186; **14**.105,
3:21	**14**.160		*270–271*
3:22	**14**.141, 153, 235;	5:6–11	**14**.*271–274*
	15.78	5:8–9	**3**.23; **14**.106; **16**.118
4:1–5	**14**.141, *245–248*	5:9	**14**.146, 158
4:3–4	**14**.145	5:12–14	**14**.159
4:3	**10**.47; **14**.165	5:12	**14**.143, *274–276*
4:4	**14**.158	5:13	**3**.4, 72; **11**.170;
4:5	**14**.141; **16**.132		**14**.160, *276–279*;
4:6	**6**.35; **14**.235, *236–243,*		**15**.18, 131, 138
	248–249	5:14	**14**.148, *279–281*
4:7a	**14**.123, 139, 140, *249–*		
	251		
4:7b–8	**14**.*251–253*	*2 Peter*	
4:8–9	**14**.124		
4:9–10	**14**.*254–256*	1:1	**14**.145, *291–294*
4:9	**7**.123; **8**.167; **12**.81;	1:2	**14**.*294–296*
	15.149	1:3–7	**14**.*296–305*
4:10	**14**.177	1:4, 5–8	**14**.283
4:11	**14**.159, *256–257*	1:8–11	**14**.*305–307*
4:12–5:11	**14**.160	1:9	**14**.283
4:12–13	**14**.*257–258*	1:10	**15**.177
4:12	**14**.146, 158	1:12–15	**14**.*307–309*
4:13	**14**.139, 141, 159;	1:16–18	**14**.*309–311*
	16.22	1:16	**14**.122
4:14–16	**14**.*258–260*	1:19–21	**14**.*311–314*
4:14, 16	**9**.12; **14**.155, 158	1:20	**14**.283
4:17–19	**14**.*260–262*	2	**15**.168f
4:17	**13**.32; **14**.139, 141	2:1	**14**.*314–318*; **16**.177
4:18	**14**.141	2:2–3	**14**.*318–319*
4:19	**14**.146	2:2, 3	**14**.283
5:1–4	**14**.*262–270*	2:4–11	**14**.*320–330*
5:1–3	**14**.160	2:4–5	**3**.34; **14**.237, 240, 283

3:13	**15**.16
3:14–17	**15**.12
3:14–15	14.227
3:16	**15**.14
3:19–24a	**15**.*85–88*
3:19	14.133
3:21	**15**.44
3:22	**15**.17, 115
3:23	**15**.12, 17
3:24	**15**.15
3:24b–4:1	**15**.*88–92*
4:1–7	**15**.91f
4:1–3	16.63
4:1	**15**.5, 44
4:2–3	5.13, 65, 223; **15**.7, 14, *92–94*
4:2	**15**.142
4:3	11.213; **15**.61, 119, 129; **17**.62
4:4–6	**15**.*94–96*
4:4–5	**15**.16, 52
4:7–21	**15**.*96–101*
4:7–12	**15**.17
4:7–10	**15**.13
4:7–8	**15**.12
4:7	14.173; **15**.44
4:9	**15**.15
4:10–12	**15**.12
4:10	**15**.14
4:11	**15**.139
4:13	**15**.15
4:14	5.171; **15**.15
4:15, 16	**15**.13
4:20–21	**15**.12, 17
4:20	14.227; **15**.32
5:1–2	**15**.*102–103*
5:1	**15**.13
5:2	**15**.17
5:3–4a	**15**.*103–105*

5:4	14.173; **15**.16
5:4b–5	**15**.*105–106*
5:5	**15**.13
5:6–8	**15**.*106–111*
5:6	**15**.9, 14
5:7	5.53; **15**.110
5:9–10	5.197; **15**.*111–112*
5:11–13	**15**.*113–114*
5:11–12	**15**.15
5:14–15	**15**.*114–116*
5:16–17	**15**.*116–121*
5:18–20	**15**.*121–123*
5:18	14.172; **15**.17
5:19	**15**.16
5:21	**15**.52, *123–125*

2 John

1–3	**15**.*137–140*
1	5.23; **15**.18, 138
4–6	**15**.*140–141*
4–5	**15**.130f
4	**15**.129f, 138
6	**15**.130
7–11	**15**.131
7–9	**15**.*141–144*
7	**15**.61, 129; **17**.62
8	**15**.130, 138
10–13	**15**.*144–145*
10	**15**.130, 138
12	**15**.129, 130, 138
13	14.160; **15**.130

3 John

1–4	**15**.*147–148*
1	5.23, 44

---

11 Phil, Col, Thes
12 Tim, Tit, Phlm
13 Heb
14 Jas, Pet
15 John, Jude
16 Rev, v.1
17 Rev, v.2

D

INDEX OF SUBJECTS AND PLACES

11 Phil, Col, Thes
12 Tim, Tit, Phlm
13 Heb
14 Jas, Pet
15 John, Jude
16 Rev, v.1
17 Rev, v.2

Asiarch **7**.3, 140
Aspasia **1**.155
Ass, symbol of **2**.243; **3**.264; **4**.240; **6**.118
Associations, Roman **12**.165f
Assos **7**.150
Assyria **1**.58; **3**.193; **11**.111; **16**.8; **17**.136f
Assyrians **1**.73, 75; **2**.281; **5**.149; **6**.120; **7**.65; **9**.131; **13**.164; **14**.37; **16**.3; **17**.53
Astrology **1**.26; **7**.66; **8**.118; **9**.47; **10**.35; **11**.95f, 134, 137; **12**.182
Astronomy **5**.57
Atheism **1**.207; **8**.49; **11**.197; **16**.80
Athenaeum **12**.124
Athens **1**.154, 333; **2**.80; **3**.279; **7**.119, 130–133; **8**.19; **9**.1, 49f, 119, 132, 164; **10**.162, 174; **12**.38, 88, 210; **13**.89; **14**.298
  Stoa Poikile of **3**.279
Athenians **6**.119; **8**.202; **10**.34, 108f; **12**.106; **17**.103
Atonement
  Day of **1**.142, 146, 233; **2**.243, 391; **3**.58, 365; **4**.223, 288; **6**.210; **7**.182; **10**.129; **13**.3, 18, 84, 96, 97–101
  Jewish **1**.52, 142, 187f, 233; **3**.258; **4**.266; **12**.9, 18f, 43, 127; **13**.98–101; **16**.177f
Attalia **7**.97
Attalus **16**.28
Augustan cohort **7**.181
'Authorities' **10**.182; **15**.166
Authority **1**.75, 133–135; **4**.243f;

6.4f; **16**.127f
Avarice **2**.331f, 335
Azariyeh **6**.102

Baal **1**.58; **4**.126; **8**.120, 144; **10**.47
  prophets of **1**.64; **4**.48; **6**.143; **16**.106
  worship of **2**.134; **3**.192; **4**.17; **16**.105f
Baal-peor **16**.67
Baaras **4**.51
Babylon **1**.13, 163; **5**.149; **14**.277; **15**.18–20, 131, 138; **16**.8, 36; **17**.2, 88, 153, 161, 211
  carpets of **9**.2
  coverlets of **17**.160
  deportation of Jews **11**.93; **14**.37f
  doom song of **17**.149, 150
  exile of Jews in **6**.22, 117; **11**.111
  fall of **17**.110, 128, 166
  symbolic use of **14**.276–278; **16**.15; **17**.63, 134, 136, 167, 168, 209
Babylonians **2**.281; **3**.193; **6**.121; **7**.11; **11**.212; **14**.37; **16**.3; **17**.53, 80
  and astrology **16**.153, 155
  and creation **17**.58, 198
  empire of **5**.185
  legends of **15**.61; **17**.77, 133
  religion of **16**.153
Balaam **12**.194
Balance, sign of **17**.215
Balinas **3**.192
Balsam **4**.234; **9**.2; **17**.161

Ban, The 6.47; 8.124; 12.53

Banias 2.134; 3.192

Banishment 16.40–42

Baptism 5.84; 6.262; 7.69, 85;
    8.83f; 11.154f; 12.169;
    13.53f; 14.243–245, 247f;
    15.89, 109
  of adults 10.32; 12.135;
    14.306
  and anointing 15.70f
  and confession 3.14; 5.iii, 83;
    10.32
  for the dead 11.152f
  and enlightenment 15.119
  with fire 1.50f
  by immersion 8.208; 12.86
  of infants 8.83; 11.140; 13.53
  and instruction 8.89f
  'into Christ' 9.16; 14.67
  and kiss of peace 14.280f
  Jewish 1.59f; 3.14, 255; 5.79;
    7.69; 8.84; 10.31f
  of John 1.47, 50; 3.13, 15,
    17f
  new birth of 14.192
  oneness of 10.142
  ordained 2.278
  in Paul 10.174; 9.15; 11.139f
  and perfection 11.65
  and resurrection 12.174
  robes of 16.121
  and sealing 17.23
  sermon of 14.160
  symbolism of 5.180; 6.141f;
    13.56

Barbarians 10.113; 11.155

Barley 3.323; 9.80, 150; 17.7

Barley-bread 3.159; 5.5, 202

Barriers 10.113f; 11.155f;
    12.64f

Baskets 2.127; 3.158, 184; 5.203

Basket, The 7.51; 12.85

Batanaea 3.53

Baths, public 1.144

Bear, symbolism of 17.88

Beast, The 17.47, 86–95, 138–
    142, 147, 184
  number of 17.100–102
  second 17.97f

Beatitudes, The 1.88–118; 4.5,
    76f

Beds, eastern 5.180

Beggars 7.32

Behemoth 1.216, 303; 17.77

Belief 3.227; 15.112
  and action 11.105
  certainty of 1.75, 352f; 8.181;
    9.130; 10.183; 11.41, 210;
    12.241; 13.128; 15.121–123
  and confession 8.139
  disturbed 3.123f
  and the Gospel 3.26
  impossibility of 3.317
  'in Christ' 5.44f, 135, 213;
    6.153
  Pauline 8.21
  Protestant 2.139
  purity of 12.153f
  restatement of 5.7
  unchangeability of 14.350
  uniformity of 12.241
  variety of 4.179; 14.73

Beloved Disciple, The 5.18–20;
    6.145

Benedictine Order, The 14.257

Benedictus, The 4.4

Benefactor, The 4.267

Benevolence 1.173; 10.164

Benjamin, tribe of **11**.58; **14**.31

Beroea **7**.119, 129; **8**.19; **11**.47, 73, 86, 181; **12**.22

Beryl **17**.159, 214, 215

Bethany **2**.238, 329, 331, 338; **3**.263f, 269, 324; **4**.142; **6**.80, 102, 108f

Bethany beyond Jordan **5**.6

Bethel **6**.53, 79

Bethesda **5**.177

Bethlehem **1**.23–25, 31, 37; **3**.65, 149; **4**.21; **5**.243, 252; **7**.68

Beth-peor **2**.159

Bethphage **2**.238; **3**.263, 324

Bethsaida **2**.11–13; **3**.27; **4**.117; **5**.6, 201

Bethsaida Julias **5**.201, 206, 225

Bethulia **13**.164

Bethzatha **5**.177

Betrothal, Jewish **1**.19; **4**.12

Bible

availability of **4**.151

criticism of **1**.4; **10**.64

divisions of **3**.299; **9**.6, 223

honesty of **7**.44

importance of **10**.90

inspiration of **4**.8

order of books **2**.298

power of **3**.13; **8**.178

revelation and **6**.195

study of **8**.195f

understanding of **4**.70f

unity of **9**.192f

use of **5**.198; **12**.100

Binding and loosing **2**.145f, 182, 189

Birmingham **15**.162

Birth, Jewish **4**.17

Bishops **12**.3, 69–72; **14**.139;

16.54, 104

Bithynia **7**.19, 121; **12**.99; **14**.137, 144f, 160f, 166; **16**.17

Bitterness **1**.110, 145, 174f, 202, 247, 392; **2**.32, 119, 247f, 288, 340; **3**.236, 243, 277; **4**.27, 116, 168, 283, 285; **6**.49; **9**.34, 226, 239, 267; **10**.90, 140, 157, 159; **11**.80; **12**.65, 128, 154, 162, 188; **13**.132; **14**.91f, 97, 173; **15**.32

Black Sea **17**.161

Blamelessness **10**.78f; **11**.43

Blasphemy **1**.324; **2**.315, 355, 357; **3**.175, 279, 321, 351; **5**.244; **6**.76; **7**.50, 61f; **12**.187; **15**.112; **17**.89, 94

Blessings **1**.370; **12**.24; **16**.180; **17**.28

Blindness **1**.349; **3**.35, 189

Blood

and covenants **2**.342

and Jerusalem Covenant **7**.116

sanctity of **2**.112; **3**.332; **17**.10

shedding of **13**.107f

sprinkling of **14**.169f

symbolism of **5**.224; **13**.131

uncleanness of **1**.346

Blood-feuds **1**.164

Boasting **8**.38; **12**.185–187; **14**.114

in Christ **11**.56; **16**.83

Body **1**.217; **3**.42, 105, 315; **8**.156; **9**.55–57, 85f; **10**.162f; **12**.119

Egyptian doctrine of **1**.321

and Gnostics **11**.98; **12**.7, 30; **15**.11

---

and Greeks **5**.64; **9**.55, 58, 140, 204

intestines **11**.18

spiritual **9**.141, 157–159, 204f

temple of Holy Spirit **8**.156f; **9**.33f, 56; **12**.96

as a text **14**.308

Boils, plague of **17**.125

Booths **2**.169

Boredom **12**.259; **15**.100

Bottomless Pit, The **17**.47

Bounty, The **3**.13

Bow, sign of **17**.4

Boy's Brigade **6**.185

Branding **16**.135; **17**.99

Bread **1**.23, 199; **2**.79

bond of **9**.91

breaking of **4**.295; **7**.149

daily **1**.390

of God **2**.127; **3**.185; **5**.215f; **16**.95

of heaven **3**.179

of Last Supper **4**.265

of life **1**.215; **2**.124–128; **5**.10, 216, 218

of the Presence **4**.70

unleavened **2**.79; **3**.332

Britain **1**.113; **2**.87; **3**.177; **9**.121; **12**.222; **17**.140

Brotherhood, Christian **3**.249; **9**.13; **11**.103f

Bull, sign of **17**.214

Burden, definition of **1**.310; **2**.22; **4**.60, 156; **10**.52f

Burial, eastern **1**.345; **17**.197

of Gentiles **3**.337

Jewish **1**.313f; **2**.372; **3**.323f, 366; **4**.289; **6**.88

mistaken **4**.111

Buskins **16** 115

Caesar

household of **8**.212; **11**.87

symbolic use **3**.284; **4**.247

worship of **1**.114, 391; **6**.182f; **16**.15–20, 90f; **17**.63, 89, 93, 95, 98–100, 131f, 141, 184

Caeserea **2**.135, 358, 363; **4**.2; **7**.138

Caesarea Philippi **1**.65; **2**.133–135, 157; **3**.191f, 209, 251, 262, 324; **4**.31, 112, 263, 280; **7**.171; **14**.5

capital city **6**.238, 243

church of **7**.6

fortress of **2**.143

and Paul **7**.73, 76

Roman H.Q. **7**.79, 167

Calvary **2**.160; **4**.3; **6**.251

Camel **2**.217, 294; **4**.229

Cana **1**.41; **5**.5f, 9, 91, 95–99, 174

Canaanites **1**.73; **2**.121; **13**.90

Cannibalism **1**.113; **4**.258; **14**.203; **16**.80

Canon, The **14**.5, 249

Capernaum **1**.71, 74, 133, 301, 307f, 326, 331, 345; **2**.11–13; **3**.29, 39, 41, 46, 49, 52f; **3**.176f; **4**.49, 86; **5**.106, 174, 201, 208

Cappadocia **14**.137, 144, 160, 166

Cappadocians **12**.242

Caria **16**.28

Carmel, Mount **1**.64; **3**.52, 176; **4**.48, 126

Carnelian **16**.152; **17**.214, 215

Carolina, North **3**.13

Carousing 10.49
Carthage 2.364; 11.50; 13.192
    Council of 12.234
Carthaginians 6.250
Caspis 13.160
Cassia 17.161
Casting lots 7.17
Castration 10.44; 13.193
Catholic Epistles 14.137
Cayster, river 7.140; 12.184
Celibacy 2.208; 14.20; 15.9;
    17.106
Cenchraea 7.133, 138; 9.2, 186
Censoriousness 8.182f
Censuses 4.20f
Centurions 1.300f; 4.84; 7.79
Chalcedon 17.213
Chalcedony 17.213, 215
Chamber of the Silent 1.188
Chance 1.89, 207; 7.14
Character 1.242; 8.74; 17.114
Chariots 17.162
Charity 1.170; 3.229, 277; 4.109,
    209; 9.118; 10.139; 13.199
Charm 7.56; 9.121; 10.9
Chastity 1.155; 2.208; 3.237f;
    4.211; 7.116; 8.90; 9.43;
    10.46, 161f; 11.97, 150f;
    12.39, 76; 17.106
Cheerfulness 2.124
Cherubim 8.117; 13.17, 96f;
    16.157f; 17.171
Cherubs 16.157
Childbirth 1.320; 4.24f
Child exposure 10.176
Childlessness 4.10, 283; 9.61;
    10.41
Children 2.174–178; 10.175–
    178; 11.161f

and angels 3.35
'of the bridechamber' 1.335;
    3.59; 4.64
care of 1.399f; 2.81
'of God' 1.109; 15.73, 81f
and Greeks 8.39; 10.34;
    12.110
and Jews 10.33f; 12.199
and Romans 10.34
Chiliasm 17.184
China 17.160
Chios 7.150
Chislew, Month of 6.69
Choice 1.277; 8.29
Chorazin 2.11–13; 4.134
Chorus, Greek 8.202
Chosen People, The 1.15, 60;
    2.264; 4.25; 5.79; 6.63;
    7.4, 52f; 8.119, 145; 10.18;
    11.156, 192; 14.166, 167, 169,
    198f, 291; 17.84
Christianity 1.50, 88f, 111–115,
    120, 167f, 172f, 286, 357, 391;
    2.66, 77, 79–81, 138, 230f,
    267; 3.64, 99f, 145, 244f,
    262, 316; 4.15f, 43, 58, 101,
    120, 170, 208, 297; 6.288;
    8.139, 167; 9.32, 121; 11.13f,
    40; 12.40, 100; 14.59, 296,
    298
adventure of 1.374, 396f;
    2.323; 3.77; 4.194f, 270
apologetic of 5.132f, 173
basis of 2.219
the Christian 1.30, 291; 3.155;
    4.183, 295; 7.161f; 8.87;
    9.13f, 148–154; 12.160–163,
    190–194, 246–256; 14.173,
    267, 296; 16.22

---

and the Cross 1.95, 214, 287,
395; 2.107, 151f, 220; 4.121;
9.170, 200
and democracy 9.265; 10.45;
13.200
foolishness of 5.49; 9.16–20
growth of 3.125, 208f; 5.26;
8.213; 10.151; 14.36f
immortality of 12.168
Jewish 2.170; 5.10; 10.19;
14.22, 41; 15.6
name of 7.90
neutrality of 4.148
purifying influence 3.12f
revolutionary 7.128
and society 2.81, 83
task of 4.181f
universality of 12.23f, 55–57;
13.92f; 15.40; 16.178; 17.16
'The Way' 7.139
Christmas tree 1.35; 17.159
Christmonger 11.190
Christology 2.138; 4.120, 137;
5.224; 11.100
Chrysolite 17.214f
Chrysoprase 17.214
Church 1.6, 7, 43f; 2.89f; 6.273;
14.286; 16.104, 173; 17.170
assembly of God 12.88
attendance at 1.107, 121;
2.270
as body of Christ 2.183;
8.159; 9.95, 108, 112–116;
10.67, 92–94, 141; 11.120
as bride of Christ 5.143;
9.246; 14.102, 276; 15.131;
16.108; 17.76, 172–174, 208,
229
and buildings 9.167; 11.171f;

17.216
as a building 2.141; 8.192;
10.119
catholicity of 17.210f
a democracy 9.265; 13.200
divisions of 9.8, 13–16, 30, 34;
10.48; 11.182; 12.265;
14.225f; 15.200
flock of God 6.62f
function of 14.198f
growth of 3.110–112; 5.7;
7.9ff; 12.91; 14.145
house churches 11.73
household of God 12.88;
13.32
inclusivism of 1.266f, 288;
8.197–200; 9.34f, 100f;
16.154
importance of 4.181
indestructibility of 2.144
and Jesus 2.139–146; 11.120–
122; 17.85
leadership of 7.91; 8.162;
9.116, 166; 10.145–150;
12.69–86, 98, 99f; 12.101–
104, 117f; 13.194f; 15.194
membership of 2.155; 3.191;
4.131, 221; 12.118
nature of 2.142; 7.30f; 9.21;
14.195–197
organization of 9.133f;
11.129, 131; 12.3; 14.26,
139f
and Paul 8.159; 11.104
and Peter 2.139–146; 14.154
pillars of 14.10
services of 12.100; 16.26
as temple of God 9.33
unity of 2.311; 3.83; 6.65,

75, 190, 215, 217f; 7.92, 145, 148; 8.3, 196f, 198, 205; 9.9, 108, 113, 116, 157, 162; 10.114f, 116f, 119, 141–143, 149; 11.7, 30, 31, 33f, 71; 12.272; 13.144; 14.224–226; 16.61

universality of 6.288; 7.145; 9.35; 16.174

weakness of 1.269; 2.166

and women 9.96–100

younger churches 12.2

Church of the Nativity 1.24f

Chuthites 5.150

Cilicia 7.73, 119; 9.2

Cilicians 12.242

Cinnamon 17.161f

Circumcision 4.24; 5.241f; 7.69; 8.65f; 10.107; 11.135

and the Church 7.112–118

Ishmaelite 11.57

and Paul 7.120; 9.251; 10.16f, 43, 56; 11.55f, 138–140

and proselytes 3.14

spiritual 11.55

symbolism of 8.125; 11.55, 139

Citizenship 2.170f, 273f; 3.287; 4.248; 8.173f; 11.69; 12.258–260; 14.159

dual 9.206

of the kingdom 11.29f; 14.201

Roman 9.4; 11.20

state and church 2.132; 3.287; 8.170–174; 14.205f

Citrus wood 17.160

City of the gods 17.214

City of Palms 4.234

Class-distinctions 8.212; 10.19; 14.47, 64f

Cleansing 2.110–117; 3.164; 10.47; 14.107f

spiritual 4.150; 6.19; 8.120; 15.30f; 17.31f

symbol of 7.69; 14.170

Cleopatra's Needle 14.250

Clothing

aprons 7.143

cloaks 1.167; 2.367; 3.142; 12.219

fine linen 1.239; 4.213; 16.143f; 17.160

girdles 1.367; 2.367; 3.142; 4.285; 7.143

leprous 3.144

Jewish 2.367; 3.141f, 362; 4.285; 6.253

rending of 1.342; 3.134

robes 3.130, 299f; 4.167, 205, 285; 16.45

shawls 4.113

tassels 1.346f; 2.286f; 3.299; 4.113

'travelling-dress' 6.89

turbans 2.367; 3.142; 4.202, 285

veils 9.97f

Clouds 2.161

Cocks 2.346; 6.229

cock-crow, the 2.346f; 3.352; 6.230

Coffins 4.62

Cohort 7.79

Coins

Jewish 1.389; 2.273; 3.286, 302; 4.171f, 241; 5.109

Roman 17.99

106; 6.69f

Defilement 3.171–175

Degeneration, spiritual 12.213

Deism 3.315

Deliverance 8.59; 9.23; 10.81f

Delphic oracles 14.349; 16.105, 114

Democracy 2.278; 3.227; 4.177; 9.265; 10.45; 11.182; 13.200; 14.206

Demons 1.289, 319–321, 366; 2.35, 112; 3.32, 34f, 71, 117–120, 225; 4.50, 54, 107f, 125f; 5.178; 9.72, 75, 91f; 10.92, 99; 11.96; 12.90f, 92; 15.89; 17.47, 176
  demon-possession 1.289, 308, 320–322; 2.35; 3.34–36, 71f, 115, 118–120; 4.50; 9.258

Dependence, spiritual 2.176; 9.198

Deposit, spiritual 12.4, 138f, 151–153

Depression 9.85

'Depths' 8.118

Derbe 7.97, 119; 11.47

Desert 1.46; 3.34; 17.143

Desire 1.136, 148, 272; 4.233; 8.28f; 10.100, 153; 11.84, 150f; 12.37; 53, 129, 189, 256; 13.40; 14.52f, 99–101, 187, 200, 329f; 15.57

Despair 2.61–63, 70; 3.97, 108, 136; 3.209, 217; 4.100; 5.55, 169; 10.109; 11.70, 82f

Destroyer, The 17.52

Devastation, The 1.63; 3.16; 4.43

Devil, The 1.106, 226; 3.22f, 330; 6.26–29, 147; 9.76, 195f; 10.157; 12.73f; 14.94, 106, 272; 15.77; 17.58, 80–82, 84, 186, 191f, 193f, 197
  devils 1.294; 2.35, 317; 3.32; 5.2; 9.72; 12.189
  Prince of devils 1.351; 2.36; 6.31

Dialogue—form 14.28

Diamonds 17.159

Diaspora 5.246; 14.21, 36–40, 166

Difficulties 2.167; 3.276; 9.170; 12.182

Dignity 12.253

Diligence 7.45

Dill 2.293

Dion 3.124

Dionysia 14.299

Discipleship 1.123, 199, 312, 361; 2.151–155, 177, 249; 3.75, 101; 5.74, 163, 196; 6.11f, 20–22, 133, 211f; 10.124f; 12.195

Discipline 1.175, 280, 292; 2.87, 173f; 3.59, 232, 234; 11.67, 150; 9.225; 10.177f; 12.161, 193; 13.175–179; 16.145f
  of Church 2.183f, 187f; 9.44–46, 96, 136, 267; 10.149; 11.131; 12.1, 116f

Discouragement 2.311

Diseass 3.23, 44

Disloyalty 1.388; 4.121; 6.142

Disobedience 1.386; 8.38, 53; 9.193; 10.100; 13.33, 46

Disorder 9.265

Dispersion, The See Diaspora

Egypt **1**.32–36, 39, 73, 329, 331;
  3.52, 91; 4.20f, 48; **14**.38;
  16.8; **17**.2, 117, 160
  deliverance from **1**.390; 2.160
  and Early Church 3.3, 209
  'the granary of Italy' 7.181
  symbolic use of **17**.71
Egyptians **1**.321; 2.112; **17**.198
Eighteen, The **1**.192
Elder, The **15**.127
Elders
  Christian 1.377; **5**.17; **17**.19,
    91, 111, 152; **9**.110; **10**.148;
    12.3, 69–84, 115f, 158, 234–
    240; **14**.21, 26, 129f, 140,
    154, 262–268; **15**.127, 133,
    137; **16**.12
  Greek **12**.70; **14**.263
  Jewish **1**.145; 2.54, 143, 147;
    2.276, 281, 287, 362; 3.163–
    167, 279, 346, 349; 4.133,
    221, 243; **9**.49; **12**.70; **14**.21,
    26, 262f; **14**.154; **16**.153
  Twenty-four, the **14**.263;
    16.152–154, 163f, 174;
    17.170
Elect, the **14**.160, 165f
Elect Lady, the **15**.19, 129f
Election **8**.120, 122, 127, 131;
  14.169
Elements **16**.31
Emanations **5**.12, 40f; **11**.97,
  114; **12**.6, 27f; **15**.164
Emancipation, spiritual **15**.121;
  16.177
Emeralds **16**.151f; **17**.159, 213,
  215
Emmaus 4.294
Emotions 2.60: 4.150; **11**.84;

  14.75f
  seat of **9**.218f
Emperor's Day, The **16**.43
Encouragement **8**.161; **13**.122
End, The   See Last Things
Endor 4.86
Endurance **9**.123, 170, 212f;
    11.210; **12**.135, 169, 197;
    13.173; **14**.176–178; **16**.39f,
    62, 131f
Engannim **5**.147
England 2.372
Enlightenment **13**.56; **15**.119
Enmity **10**.47
Enthusiasm **1**.313
Envy 2.288; 3.175; **8**.35, 179;
    9.120, 263f; **10**.48; **13**.132;
    14.190
Ephesians, *Letter to* **10**.61–71;
    11.172, 174; **14**.139
  and *1 Peter* **14**.152–154
  and *Revelation* **16**.57–71
Ephesus **1**.378; **7**.3, 146f; **9**.6;
    10.148; **11**.91; **12**.33, 71,
    92f, 170, 184f; **16**.28, 58–61;
    17.206
  and Andrew **5**.21
  and Apollos **8**.209
  Bishop of **12**.275
  Capital of Asia **12**.155
  'Ephesian Letters'   See amulets
  'Highway of the Martyrs' **16**.58
  and John the Apostle **2**.231;
    5.6f, 17, 20, 22, 27
  and John the Elder **5**.23
  Market of Asia **16**.58
  and Paul **5**.50; **7**.119, 121,
    138, 140–144; **9**.4; **11**.47
  provenance of John's *Gospel*

| 1 Matt, v.1 | 3 Mark | 5 John, v.1 | 7 Acts | 9 Cor |
| 2 Matt, v.2 | 4 Luke | 6 John, v.2 | 8 Rom | 10 Gal, Eph |

and *Letters* 14.161; 15.18f, 123f, 137
and Roma 16.17
and Timothy 12.89, 143, 184
Ephraim 6.106
Epicureans 3.125; 7.130, 132; 13.42f; 16.84
Epilepsy 1.321; 4.125; 9.258; 10.38
Epirus 12.9, 265
Equality 12.116
Escapism 2.167; 13.72f
Esdraelon, Plain of 1.71; 4.47; 17.132
E.S.P. 1.306
Essenes 1.161, 359; 8.182; 14.127
Eternal life 2.214, 216; 5.43f, 127–129, 136f; 6.207–209; 12.228; 15.113f
Ethics 1.118, 123, 163, 272–277; 2.172, 206, 310; 3.29; 4.79f; 6.26; 9.14, 64, 68; 11.29f, 12.40, 88f, 108; 14.72, 201f; 15.17f, 82, 88; 17.107
  Greek 9.37; 11.84
  O.T. 1.165
  of reciprocal obligation 1.274; 11.160f; 14.222f
Ethiopia 7.69
  church of 14.64
  eunuch of 7.19, 63, 68f
Eunuchs 2.207
Euphrates 1.113; 5.178; 17.52f, 128, 134
  valley of 12.184
Europe 7.5, 19, 119
Evangelicals 11.23f
Evangelism 2.173; 3.191; 5.173;

9.64, 84; 11.15, 24; 12.204, 229; 16.142
Evangelists 10.147
Evasion 2.291–293; 13.73
Evil 1.70, 245f; 2.118–120; 3.174; 4.150; 8.38, 98; 13.83; 14.50, 86f, 189f
  and Belial 17.59
  definition of 8.34
  fascination of 14.297; 17.147
  influence of 6.37f
  Man of 14.328–330
  origin of 1.226; 6.216
  power of 1.225, 351, 366; 11.212f; 15.89
  root of 12.131–133
Evil One, The 1.225; 3.174, 330; 6.216; 9.196; 15.51, 55, 122; 17.82
Evolution 4.137f, 175
Example 1.124
Excellence 11.80f; 14.301
Exclusivism, Jewish 1.266; 9.48
Excommunication
  Christian 9.44–46, 48; 15.118
  Jewish 3.165; 6.45, 47; 9.61; 12.53
Exhortation 8.161
Exile 1.13, 73; 2.136
'Exiles of Eternity' 14.167f
Exorcism 1.289; 2.37–39, 166; 3.35, 37, 78, 225; 4.50f, 129, 147; 7.144
  gift of 9.110f
  and prayer 3.219
Exorcists, Order of 3.35
Expediency 2.258
Experience 5.173; 12.32
Eyes 1.351; 3.231

generous 1.245–248
  evil 6.42; 10.24
Eye-salve 16.138f

Factiousness 9.264
Failure 3.218f
Fair Havens 7.182f
Faith 1.69, 303, 340, 342; 2.75,
    120–123, 167f; 3.140, 216–
    218, 261f; 4.112; 9.143, 157;
    10.26, 183, 185; 11.171, 186;
    12.3, 52, 134, 154, 180;
    13.53, 147; 14.301; 17.34,
    210
  aristocracy of 1.304
  defence of 15.177–179
  definition of 9.78; 13.128–130
  gift of 9.109
  and love 9.118
  and miracles 1.350
  in Paul 8.21f, 61–64, 140f;
    10.23, 43; 14.349
  and prayer 3.276f; 6.180
  quaternion of 14.287
  and thought 12.33
  vicarious 1.326; 2.166; 4.63
  victory of 15.105
  and works 1.290; 14.22, 71–
    74, 76–79
Faith, The 8.21; 9.25f; 10.141f;
    11.5; 12.157f, 162; 13.49, 53–
    55; 14.182f
Falsehood 1.286–290; 10.155;
    12.194f
Family 1.393; 3.289f; 4.145f,
    212; 8.39; 12.241
Famine 17.6–8
Fasting 1.44, 179, 185, 232–238
  Jewish 1.233–236, 335; 3.58f;

  4.66, 223; 13.98
  pre-baptismal 13.54
Fatalism 11.96, 137
Fate 4.250; 6.212; 7.49; 16.167
'Father' 2.287, 361; 8.126
Fatherhood 10.129f
Favouritism 14.63
Fear 1.386, 388; 2.60; 5.45;
    6.130; 8.119; 9.207; 11.42f;
    12.127; 13.38, 121; 17.206
Fearlessness 4.160f
Feasts 1.111; 3.300, 322–324;
    4.192f, 267; 5.177, 203; 9.100
Feet-washing 6.137
Fellowship 1.384; 2.53, 142,
    146, 174, 189, 221; 3.73,
    316; 4.296; 7.30, 111, 149;
    8.161, 195–198; 9.10, 34, 99f;
    10.133; 11.14, 64, 157;
    12.118, 278; 14.195f, 208,
    281; 15.17f, 21, 30
  apostolic 9.145, 163
  with Christ 8.81f, 93f, 105;
    15.35
  with God 5.129; 13.1, 106;
    15.29, 39; 17.202–204
  with unbelievers 9.221–223
Fight, Christian 12.210–212
Fig trees 2.251f; 4.174f; 9.80
  symbolism of 2.251; 5.93
Fig-mulberry tree 4.234
Fire 1.200f; 3.234
  symbolism of 4.169; 17.117
Firkin 5.98
Firmament 16.155; 17.14
Firstborn 4.24; 8.84; 11.119;
    13.187
  slaying of 17.125
First-fruits 2.371; 4.155; 9.149–

'Friends of the Bridegroom'
5.143; 9.246
Fruits, spiritual 1.283–285;
3.271; 6.174; 10.164; 11.107
Fundamentalism 11.136
Funerals, Jewish 4.86f; 6.88f
Futility 14.187

Gabbatha 5.6; 6.245
Gad, tribe of 14.31
Gadara 1.319; 3.124f
Galatae 16.88
Galatia 4.31; 7.5, 138; 10.44;
12.184; 14.137, 144f, 160, 166
Galatians, *Letter to* 10.3–6
Galbanum 17.161
Galilee 1.39, 71–74, 80, 363f,
395; 2.12, 95, 98f, 127, 194,
343; 3.27, 37, 52, 53, 160,
176, 210; 4.3, 31, 45, 129;
7.5, 70; 8.173
revolts in 2.180; 3.229; 4.45,
172f, 278
Sea of 1.72, 76f, 308, 316f;
2.78, 125, 180; 3.115, 118,
180, 184, 187; 4.56f, 105
Games
gladiatorial 3.204
Isthmian 7.134; 9.2, 20, 85;
11.45
Marathon, the 12.210
Olympian 7.134; 9.2, 85;
11.45; 12.211; 16.83
Pan-Ionian 7.140; 11.45
Roman 2.77
of Smyrna 16.83
Torch-races 8.202
Gate, Eastern 2.142f
Gaul 2.97; 3.153; 14.144;

16.89; 17.92
Gaulonites 3.53
Gaza 3.52; 7.68
Ge 3.175
Gehenna 1.47, 139, 140f, 304,
388; 2.182f; 3.231f; 6.90;
12.67; 17.12, 47
Gehinnom 2.206; 5.162
Genealogies 1.12; 5.7; 12.6,
26, 264
General Epistles, The 14.137
Generosity 1.245–248; 8.161;
12.23, 278f
Geneva Version 1.245
Gennesaret 3.115; 4.56
Gentiles 1.6, 17, 73, 82, 363;
2.34, 114, 121f, 126f, 131,
187, 189, 224, 243f, 266, 270;
3.177; 4.6
conversion of 1.301–304; 2.71,
145; 3.283; 6.133, 283;
7.19, 88, 112–118; 8.53, 121–
123, 147–150; 10.126; 12.23f;
14.291f; 15.169; 17.216–218
and Jews 1.370; 2.80, 290;
3.178; 4.48, 140; 5.79;
10.107–110; 15.45; 16.7f
and Luke's Gospel 4.3
reception into Church 7.4,
62f; 14.10
uncleanness of 2.110, 295;
3.13f, 69, 143, 166; 6.235
Gentle, gentleness 1.98; 9.238;
10.51, 137; 11.19, 75, 158;
12.83, 135, 181, 259; 14.58,
231
Gerasa 1.320; 3.124; 4.107
Gerasenes 3.184
Gergesa 1.320

| 1 Matt, v.1 | 3 Mark | 5 John, v.1 | 7 Acts | 9 Cor |
| 2 Matt, v.2 | 4 Luke | 6 John, v.2 | 8 Rom | 10 Gal, Eph |

Gergesenes 1.319

Gerizim 2.359; 5.116, 157
  temple of 5.150

Germany 1.113; 14.221

Giants, The 3.175

Gibeonites 13.90

Gifts (talents) 1.66f; 2.67, 91;
    3.219; 4.97; 8.91, 159f;
    9.12, 116, 127; 10.81–83;
    11.127; 12.60–62, 94f;
    14.255f; 17.219
  Spiritual 9.95, 108–112, 117,
    133f, 136; 10.143–145; 14.45;
    15.90

Gifts, giving 1.169–172, 187–
    191, 357, 366; 3.302f; 4.178,
    191, 255; 5.161; 9.164,
    228–230, 232f, 234–237, 261f;
    14.44f; 15.151

Gihon 6.43

Glass 16.156

Glastonbury Thorn 2.372, 289f

Glory 5.68–70; 15.166
  crown of 16.83
  'to give glory to' 6.48

Gluttony 17.157

Gnat 2.294

Gnosticism 5.12f, 18, 40f;
    6.257f; 10.163; 11.68f, 97–
    99, 113–120, 130, 134f, 136,
    144–146; 12.6–8, 27–31, 119,
    192f, 244; 13.197; 14.284;
    15.5–12, 66, 76f, 78f, 93, 108,
    163, 171, 180; 17.106
  dualism of 12.62
  and matter 5.12, 40; 6.259;
    11.97, 114, 144; 12.6, 27
  scriptures of 12.199
  and sin 15.164

and spirit 11.97, 114; 12.30

Goat, sign of 17.215

God
  access to 10.117, 127; 13.1f,
    102
  almighty, the 16.38, 162;
    17.173
  alpha & omega 17.204
  arms of 17.85
  army of 13.17
  assembly of 12.88f
  authority of 6.6
  the beginning 17.204, 226
  the Blessed One 14.90
  breath of 7.20
  calling of 10.77; 15.177
  care of 1.217, 389f; 2.99, 173;
    4.161; 6.161
  children of 5.60–63
  city of 17.207–216
  comfort of 2.224; 11.83
  compassion of 2.127, 225;
    6.98
  consuming fire 14.188f;
    17.117
  council of 16.153
  creator 1.97; 7.132; 8.27;
    11.158; 12.94; 16.141, 164;
    17.110
  decree of 17.97
  the end 17.204f
  existence of 1.206–208
  eternity of 14.38, 163
  family of 3.112; 8.107, 124;
    10.117f; 13.17; 15.78, 102
  fatherhood of 1.200, 202–204;
    2.176, 349f; 3.249, 344; 4.74,
    143, 222, 226; 5.51, 73, 138;
    6.27, 64f; 8.107, 113f, 132f,

164; 10.35, 128–131, 142; 11.162; 12.261; 13.42; 15.73f

fear of 6.212

forbearance of 8.41f

foreknowledge of 14.169

forgiveness of 3.51f; 4.205; 10.54

foundation of 12.176

friend of 6.178

fullness of 10.65; 11.118f, 137

generosity of 1.247; 2.225; 3.282; 10.25, 76, 77

glory of 2.161, 191, 196; 3.238; 5.9, 68–70; 6.39, 100; ·7.164; 8.125; 11.41; 17.35f, 72f, 122f, 169, 202f

grace of 1.198, 287, 300; 2.31, ·268; 5.62; 6.39; 7.114; 8.5, 13, 27, 139; 9.160, 174, 211; 10.30, 94f, 127, 163; 11.17, 19, 53, 63; 12.24; 13.93, 182; 14.177; 15.96, 180, 206

greatness of 17.120

hand of 14.271

holiness of 1.62, 203, 208, 388; 2.6; 3.315; 4.225; 5.112, 214; 8.25; 9.89, 132, 174; 10.130; 13.42; 15.26, 33, 127; 16.152, 156, 162; 17.123

of hope 11.82

house of 16.153

household of 12.88; 13.119

image of 11.116–118

infinite 13.51

initiative of 5.86; 11.214

of Israel 2.126

jealousy of 14.104

joy of 4.202

judge, the 1.137, 146; 2.75, 263, 309, 324–326; 3.250; 4.220, 246; 5.187; 8.33; 9.190, 193; 11.149, 197; 12.121, 179; 13.187; 14.112, 115; 15.176, 185; 17.2, 16, 44, 57, 169, 194

justice of 1.55, 208; 2.6; 3.282, 316; 8.52, 138; 13.93

kindness of 4.201; 8.41f

kingship of 1.202, 388; 2.100, 169; 8.73, 222; 10.108; 12.17; 14.166; 15.24; 17.119

knowledge of 6.208f; 8.114; 10.91; 14.294f; 15.17, 40–43, 54

life-giver 1.256; 2.144; 5.44, 64; 9.140; 15.113

the light 6.13; 15.25f; 16.151

'the living God' 5.43; 17.21f

Lord of hosts 16.39

Lord Sabaoth 16.39

love of 1.208, 214; 2.6, 185f, 278, 367; 3.277, 316; 4.6, 114, 203, 205, 272, 288; 5.73, 137, 214; 6.55, 85, 201; 8.75–77, 112, 115–119, 153–155; 9.12, 147, 160, 190, 193; 10.9, 10, 82, 119, 124, 130, 163; 11.51, 78, 122f, 125, 187, 216; 12.29, 36, 148, 230, 261; 13.13, 58f, 93, 117, 119, 146; 14.216, 253; 15.24f, 97, 203, 207; 17.97, 142, 169

is love 9.34; 10.104; 15.17, 98

of love 11.83

1 Matt, v.1	3 Mark	5 John, v.1	7 Acts	9 Cor
2 Matt, v.2	4 Luke	6 John, v.2	8 Rom	10 Gal, Eph

Hobbies **13**.73
Holiness **2**.270; **4**.44; **8**.89;
    9.10; **10**.154; **11**.124; **12**.146;
    13.181f; **14**.188, 189f, 199
  beauty of **17**.222
  spirit of **9**.216
  way of **6**.157
Holy **8**.94; **10**.77f; **11**.10;
    12.65; **15**.176f
Holy City, The **2**.225; **4**.180
Holy Grail, The **2**.372; **4**.290
Holy Land, The **5**.59
Holy Spirit, The **1**.20–23, 48–50,
    201; **2**.39, 41–44, 83, 156;
    3.6, 17, 140; **4**.8, 13, 26, 68,
    82, 145, 286; **5**.154, 227;
    7.5, 66, 141f; **8**.101–104, 110;
    9.106; **10**.23, 141; **13**.55f;
    14.141, 313; **15**.15, 89, 101,
    108; **16**.43f
  Comforter **1**.200; **5**.5; **6**.166f;
    7.10
  coming of **5**.82–85; **7**.10, 12,
    18f; **9**.205; **14**.175, 250;
    15.70f
  and Docetics **5**.13
  earnest of **9**.177
  eternal **13**.105
  filling of **10**.166
  fruit of **10**.49–52
  gifts of **6**.284; **16**.31f, 116
  grieving of **10**.158; **13**.125
  and Jesus **3**.20f, 79f; **5**.5, 52,
    53, 250; **6**.273f; **7**.29, 42;
    9.17, 157; **10**.145; **11**.25;
    12.90; **15**.108f
  Jewish doctrine of **1**.48f;
    4.161; **5**.83f; **6**.30; **13** 166
  liberty of **9**.194

  personal **5**.252
  power of **12**.262f
  and prayer **8**.111; **15**.203
  revealer **9**.27f
  and Scripture **5**.22f, 24, 185;
    14.180, 313f
  sealing of **10**.87; **17**.23
  sevenfold **16**.31f, 116, 155
  sin against **2**.41–45; **3**.80f;
    4.161; **16**.12
  symbolism of **16**.160
  teacher **6**.170
  temple of **8**.156f; **9**.33f, 56;
    12.96
  of Truth **4**.161; **5**.24, 53, 67;
    6.18, 194–196
  and unity **11**.33f
  of wisdom **10**.90
  witness of **6**.188; **8**.107
  work of **6**.192–194; **7**.19f,
    142; **9**.189f; **10**.35; **14**.169,
    171; **16**.22; **17**.222
  and worship **11**.56
Home-life **1**.112; **5**.100f; **9**.70;
    11.199; **12**.250
Honesty **1**.119; **14**.202
Homosexuality **8**.32; **9**.53;
    12.38, 97; **15**.42, 185; **17**.140
Honey **3**.16; **9**.80
Hope **2**.63; **3**.108, 136; **4**.27f,
    57, 190, 287; **8**.108–111, 166,
    196, 198f; **9**.124, 169; **10**.91,
    110; **11**.25f, 83, 106, 125,
    186f; **12**.19–21, 154, 263;
    13.61–63, 127, 128–131, 149f;
    14.172, 183; **17**.26
  and character **8**.74f
  and faith **2**.124; **8**.21
  gospel of **3**.25

14.40; 17.116, 142

church of 3.4; 7.5, 6, 95, 101;
   7.145; 8.2; 9.228, 236

conquests of 2.281; 3.193

council of 2.145; 7.19, 112–
   118; 14.10, 23, 264, 292;
   15.169; 16.67

fall of 1.383; 2.28, 267, 300,
   302, 305–308; 3.68, 306, 309–
   311, 321; 4.173, 241, 258;
   13.167; 14.38

gate of 4.229

mountains of 2.182

new 3.197; 13.145, 186; 16.8f,
   98, 128, 135, 176; 17.199–
   202, 212

at Passover 2.238; 3.324

and the prophets 2.299

Jeshimmon 1.63; 3.16; 4.43

Jesse, stump of 1.40

Jews

defined 7.51; 8.47, 66, 127

dispersion of 1.383

and Gentile 1.17; 4.133; 5.55;
   7.52f, 80, 82, 107; 8.41, 137;
   9.49; 10.4f, 18, 85f, 92;
   11.54; 12.32; 14.26, 62

and Gnosticism 10.99

history of 2.134

ingathering of 16.8; 17.18f

pride of 11.155

problem of 8.5, 6, 119–123

rebelliousness of 8.173

religious genius of 10.86

sins of 11.191f

Jezreel, plain of 4.47

Job, *book of* 1.181; 3.134

John, *Letters of* 5.23f; 14.137;
   15.3–20, 123, 127–136; 16.165

John, *gospel of*

authorship 5.15–24, 53

and crucifixion 6.292f

discourses of 5.164f, 185;
   6.16, 86

and Ephesus 5.6

and Gnosticism 12.27

introduction 5.1–24, 42, 51,
   66, 76, 107, 185; 16.165

and Jews 5.76

judgement in 5.43, 138–140;
   6.193f

and life 5.42–46

and light 5.42, 45f, 48, 54

and love 6.85, 169, 177; 15.44

and miracles 6.39

oral preaching 5.3

order of 5.176; 6.108

paradoxes of 5.138

prologue of 5.1–75

and resurrection 5.43

size of 16.165

symbolism 4.2; 5.1; 16.160f

and truth 5.1, 9, 53f, 66–68

'witness' in 5.19, 51–53, 76

words of Jesus 5.133, 185

and the world 6.18

Jordan, river 1.58, 69, 82, 308;
   2.11, 134; 3.52, 192; 5.201

and Jewish hopes 3.185

Jordan valley 1.76, 316; 2.157

Jotapata 3.134

Joy 1.89f, 95, 116, 337; 2.267,
   376; 3.60; 4.66, 103, 230;
   6.177, 198, 214, 220; 7.65;
   8.192; 10.50; 11.13f, 50–52,
   71, 75, 109f, 189, 195; 12.163;
   14.48f, 174; 15.13, 21; 16.10

The Epistle of 11.8

12.36, 198; **14**.347; **15**.56;
16.40, 94, 123, 129; **17**.187,
196
and children 2.174–178
citizens of 2.289; **11**.29f
consummation of 1.212
entry into 2.84; **4**.229
feast of 4.195
imminence of 1.364, 381f;
2.137, 155f, 315; **3**.208
and Jewish hope 3.17, 188
and love 4.193
mystery of 3.91f
proclamation of 1.370; **7**.5,11
and repentance 1.352
signs of 4.220
sons of 1.304
stewards of 2.145
word of 15.24
yoke of 2.17
Kingdom of heaven 1.92; **2**.7f,
76, 87ff, 139–146, 169, 173,
217–219; **3**.111, 241; **4**.179,
181f, 228; **5**.127; **8**.192
Kingdom of priests 16.35, 178
King's College 12.176
King's Highway 1.45
Kingship 3.71; **4**.267; **11**.58;
15.69
spiritual 3.82f
Knowledge 1.291; **3**.104f;
8.100; **9**.109, 215; **10**.35, 82;
11.63, 99, 130; **14**.302; **15**.10
gift of 9.118
and Greeks 5.55; **8**.159; **9**.37
growth in 13.50
O.T. 8.114
responsibility of 6.186
self-knowledge 8.159; **9**.132

sexual 6.209; **15**.185
way of 5.197; **11**.18
Kranion 4.3
Krenides 11.3

Lake of Fire 17.47
Lambeth Conference 1.392
Lamentations, *Book of* 3.135
Lamps 1.85; **4**.167
Lamp of Israel 1.122
Lampstand 1.122; **2**.244
Landlords 4.208
Language, eastern 4.216; **11**.155
Laodicaea 3.320; **11**.91, 93;
12.184; **16**.28, 47, 137–139
Church of 2.218; **10**.68f;
11.127f, 171; **12**.273
and Jews 16.139
Letter to 16.136–148
Lost letter to 10.172–174;
12.273, 274
Last days, The 3.306; **14**.174;
15.59f; **16**.7, 22; **17**.5, 17
Last hour, The 15.59f
Last Supper, The 1.113; **2**.128,
338–343, 348, 372; **3**.347;
4.264–267; **5**.1, 19, 48, 204;
6.272, 292; **7**.95; **10**.84
Last Things, The 1.8; **8**.151;
14.250; **16**.167; **17**.13, 29, 55
as Terror 17.15–17
Last Trumpet, The 10.165
Laughter 4.66, 195
Lausanne 2.359
Law, and Greeks 1.144; **12**.35
Law, Jewish 1.6, 47, 52, 80, 126–
131, 134, 166, 208, 268, 284,
337, 356; **2**.8f; **3**.31, 163,
293, 4.59–61; **5**.120f, 197;

8.126; 13.66; 14.69
books of 1.347
burden of 2.17; 10.6
ceremonial 1.286; 2.290;
4.250
of freedom 14.7
function of 10.29
and Gospel 1.131–133
homes of 1.242
inadequacy of 1.366–368;
10.20f, 26; 11.61–63
and the Kingdom 3.17
oral 1.127, 129; 2.114, 128;
3.32, 164, 289; 4.250; 8.44–
46
personified 1.52
and religion 10.36
royal 14.68
scribal 1.127; 2.128; 3.57
simplicity of 2.117
son of 4.29; 10.33f
study of 5.124
tables of 13.96
use of 8.57
and wisdom 5.154
written 2.114
yoke of 2.17
Law, moral 1.201, 208; 10.55
Law, Roman 2.74, 372
Lawlessness 1.221; 8.90; 12.37
Lawless One, The 11.212
Laying-on of hands 7.66f;
12.117f; 13.54f
Lazar-houses 3.45
Learning 1.97; 3.114; 4.29;
13.48
discipline of 17.224
Leaven 1.7; 2.79, 130–132, 339;
3.187f, 225, 332; 4.50, 180–

182, 262; 9.45; 10.44
Lechaeum 7.133; 9.2
Legalism 1.128, 311f; 2.132,
189, 209f; 3.32, 168; 4.157,
159, 178; 5.121; 8.64; 9.160;
10.24, 37, 42; 11.96, 189;
12.6, 7
and Jesus 8.138, 140f; 10.26,
115
Legalists 2.282, 292; 8.180;
9.15
Leontopolis 14.39
Leopard, symbolism of 17.88, 93
Lepers 1.293, 296, 365; 3.238
cleansing of 1.299f; 14.170
Leprosy 1.295–299; 3.35, 43–46;
4.217f
Lesbos 7.150
Letters, ancient 8.x–xi; 10.62;
11.12
of commendation 8.207;
9.185
of credit 16.138
Leviathan 1.216, 303; 4.192;
17.58, 77
Levi, tribe of 14.31
Levites 1.26; 2.293; 4.155, 224;
5.76f; 6.36; 9.80; 13.8, 76;
17.34
Libations 1.111f; 11.46
Liberality 1.245
Liberation 8.59; 10.81f
Liberty 1.117, 168; 7.105;
8.179, 192f; 9.76, 134, 214;
11.68f, 189; 12.192; 13.196;
14.207; 16.68
of conscience 3.287
law of 14.60, 70
of speech 3.227; 11.26;

questioning 2.102; 4.124; 10.90; 16.117

shut 1.361; 2.59f, 323; 4.68, 100; 5.131, 192, 198; 6.21, 170, 245; 12.101; 13.49

and truth 1.338–340

and universe 1.207

Ministry, Christian 1.121; 4.115; 9.84; 10.90; 12.100f, 128, 217

in Early Church 9.134; 10.146f; 11.171; 15.132–136; 16.12

Mint 2.293

Miracles 1.289, 300, 304–307, 350; 2.171, 237; 3.218; 4.57; 5.119; 6.100, 101; 7.32f, 193; 9.109f

Mirrors 9.125; 13.95; 14.59; 17.140, 159

Misenum 7.190

Missionary task 1.356f; 2.291; 6.67; 11.44; 16.129

Mites 3.302; 4.171

Mithradates 14.144

Mithraism 5.222; 17.33

Mitylene 7.150

Moab 2.159

Moabites 9.88

Mohammedans 1.194, 196, 233; 3.168, 291; 9.118

Molech 1.58, 141; 2,183; 3.231; 7.60

Monarchy 10.45

Money 1.252; 2.84; 4.164f

love of 3.328; 12.131–133, 184

money-changers 2.244f; 4.241; 5.109f

Monks 1.149

Monotheism 3.295; 6.161

Months, Jewish 2.169; 6.69; 10.36

Morality

of world 8.26f; 11.152; 13.108; 17.86

pollution 12.37f; 14.173

sexual 3.240; 15.199f

Moravian Church 14.131

Moriah, Mount 3.308

Morning Star, The 16.110f

Mote 1.85

Motherhood 12.68f

Motives 1.185, 342; 2.173; 9.37, 174f, 209; 12.120, 252f

Mourning 1.93, 233, 343f; 3.132–135; 4.86f; 6.88f

spiritual 14.108f

Murder 1.135f, 379; 3.173, 238; 7.166; 8.35, 176; 12.38

and the Jews 2.297f; 4.211

Muslims See Mohammedans

Mustard 2.75f; 3.109f; 4.178f

Myra 7.181

Myrrh 1.32; 17.161f

Mysia 7.19; 16.28

Mystery 2.64, 66; 3.91; 5.226; 9.26, 94, 125, 170; 10.83; 16.53; 17.109, 143f

'Secret' 11.126, 130

Mystery Religions 2.65f; 3.91; 5.126f, 222; 8.84f; 10.113; 12.67f, 262; 14.25, 295f, 310f; 15.42, 70; 17.33

Mysticism 6.175; 9.256

Nablus 5.147

Nain 4.86

Names 6.5, 210; 13.60; 15.87

1 Matt, v.1	3 Mark	5 John, v.1	7 Acts	9 Cor
2 Matt, v.2	4 Luke	6 John, v.2	8 Rom	10 Gal, Eph

5.14; 6.221
Olympus 17.133
Onycha 17.161
Opal 17.159
Ophites 15.164
Optimism 2.230; 3.304; 6.32
Opportunity 2.330; 6.40, 87;
    8.165; 11.24; 13.50; 16.149
Order 1.207; 5.57
Orontes 7.89, 97
Orphic religion 14.25, 87f;
    16.29f
Orthodoxy 3.316; 4.140; 11.105,
    113; 12.4, 31; 14.349;
    16.62–64, 117
  frozen 11.132
  Jewish 3.48; 4.140
Ostia 17.164
Ovens 1.121, 257; 4.165
Overseers See elders
Ox, symbolism of 5.1; 16.159

Pacifism 1.175
Pain 1.201, 354f; 2.39
Palaia Kaumene 17.45
Palestine 1.72, 298f, 307f; 3.37,
    46, 52, 53, 124, 208; 5.59,
    146f; 6.237f; 7.11, 15;
    17.5, 116
Palm, sign of 17.26f
Pamphylia 3.3; 7.97
Pan 2.134; 3.192
Panias 2.134; 3.192
Panium 2.134f
Pantheism 15.161
Papacy 2.139; 15.63; 17.100
Paphos 7.97, 100
Papyrus 1.330; 7.86; 8.x; 9.223;
    11.142; 15.127; 16.165f

Parables
  defined 2.54–56, 261; 3.85,
    90, 281; 4.146
  of dragnet 2.78; 12.179
  of the friend 4.4, 222
  of great feast 1.333
  of hidden treasure 2.79, 83–86
  of the Kingdom 2.79
  of last judgment 1.179f
  of the leaven 2.79
  of the lost sheep 4.200
  of the mustard seed 2.78
  of the pounds 4.172
  of the prodigal son 3.14; 4.5;
    16.116
  of the rich man 4.5
  of the sheep and goats 17.195
  of the sower 2.55–63, 78;
    4.98–102; 14.57, 189
  of the talents 1.184; 2.84,
    321–324; 4.172
  of the ten virgins 14.300
  of the unjust judge 4.4
  of the wheat and tares 2.78;
    12.179
  of the wicked husbandman
    2.69; 3.89f; 14.166, 194
Paradise 1.52; 4.286f; 6.34,
    153f; 9.257; 13.134; 16.69f,
    84, 122; 17.199, 220
Parchment 16.88
Parent-slayers 12.38
Parthia 15.63; 17.63, 147
Parthians 3.103, 320; 15.18;
    17.4, 53, 129, 141, 184
Partnership 11.17
Passion 1.137; 3.231; 4.106;
    9.158; 10.159; 11.151; 12.191
Passover 1.41; 2.79, 238f, 245,

296, 328, 339–342; 3.260,
270, 331–334, 336–339; 4.4,
9, 29, 232, 241, 262f, 265;
5.106, 108, 177, 201, 228;
6.115, 146f, 235; 7.21, 94,
148, 150; 9.149f; 10.36;
13.158; 14.185
and Bethany 3.264
Christian· 9.44
and Elijah 2.136; 3.147
and Greeks 6.119
Lamb of 2.339, 341; 5.80f;
6.259, 261; 14.244
the Last 3.331–334
and Messiah 2.136; 3.338
and the Preparation 2.374
at spring-time 2.105, 252;
3.160f
and trials 2.353; 4.280; 6.241
Pastoral Epistles, the 12.1–13
Pastors 10.147f; 11.194–196
Paternity 10.129
Patience 1.78f; 2.63, 167; 3.108,
113; 4.220; 8.42; 9.119f,
216; 10.50, 138; 11.75, 83,
108, 158; 12.135, 196; 13.46,
144f; 14.43, 124f, 303
Patmos 5.17; 16.14, 40–42, 50,
156; 17.127
Patriarchs 8.149; 13.148;
16.154; 17.170
Testament of See Index VI
Paulinism 8.44; 9.204; 11.11;
13.1
paradox of 10.104f
pillars of 8.19–23
quintessence of 10.70f
Peace 1.97, 108, 112, 158; 3.213,
236; 4.230; 5.87, 93; 6.171;

7.114f; 8.169f, 191f, 199;
10.50, 76, 140, 185; 11.12,
206; 12.23f, 180; 13.72–74;
14.95, 294; 16.29; 17.5
angel of 17.40
Gospel of 3.25
King of 13.69
kiss of 1.113; 4.94; 8.169;
9.63, 168; 11.189; 14.148,
279–281
meaning of 4.19; 10.9
and Messiah 5.77
The Peace 9.168
and righteousness 13.72
way of 10.26
Peace-makers 1.108; 3.140f;
13.180f
Pearl 2.86f; 17.159
Pella 1.82; 3.124; 17.85
Peloponnese 9.1
Penitence 1.95, 142, 234; 6.274;
14.347; 17.34
and forgiveness 3.81
Pentateuch, The 1.127; 2.275f,
277, 281; 3.31, 163, 289
and Samaritans 5.159
Pentecost 2.42, 145, 156; 3.80;
5.83, 252; 6.115; 10.36;
15.109
Day of 7.18
Feast of 3.323; 4.9; 5.177;
7.21, 150f, 157
People, importance of 1.251;
2.173; 3.64; 4.174, 177;
8.12; 14.208
People of the land 3.56; 4.199;
5.253; 13.93
Peroea 1.82; 2.95; 4.31
Perfection, moral 1.177; 9.26;

14.40, 144f; **16**.28, 125, 137, 139

Piety **1**.185, 325; **12**.239; **14**.303f

Phylacteries **2**.286; **3**.295; **4**.140; **17**.99

Pilatus, Mount **2**.359

Pilgrims **3**.273; **13**.149; **14**.144, 167; **16**.91

Jewish **3**.324

Pillars **16**.134

Pisidia **14**.144

Pitiless **8**.39

Pity **1**.103, 354; **4**.214; **11**.157; **14**.96, 227

Plagues **2**.339; **17**.14, 44, 71, 124f, **17**.125–128, 130, 134

Platonism **8**.173f; **12**.2, 88; **16**.55; **17**.199

Pleasure **1**.94, 238, 240, 391; **2**.207; **4**.195; **6**.23; **8**.28f, 31, 96, 189; **9**.52, 76; **10**.100; **12**.161, 188, 191; **13**.129, 184; **14**.98–101, 331

Plutocracy **10**.45

Poetry **5**.22, 27

Polygamy **12**.76

Pomegranate **9**.80

Pompeii **3**.320, 359

Pontifical Letters, The **12**.1

Pontus **8**.209; **14**.137, 144, 160, 166

Poor, The **1**.90–92, 241; **3**.6, 326; **4**.5; **14**.61, 66f

Possessiuns **1**.239f, 249–254; **2**.215f; **3**.122, 244, 247f; **4**.164f, 194, 206, 228f; **9**.120, 235; **12**.129f, 185; **14**.255f

Postal system, Roman **10**.62;

16.101, 129

Poverty **1**.90–92; **2**.208; **3**.122f; **12**.130; **14**.66f; **16**.78

Power **3**.219; **8**.200; **9**.110

Powers **8**.117f; **9**.92; **10**.92, 182; **11**.96

Praetorium **3**.359; **7**.167

guard of **7**.193; **11**.20f

Praetor Urbanus **8**.188

Praise **8**.47, 197; **17**.169

Prayer **1**.179, 191–232, 270–272; 357; **2**.123f, 190f, 255–257, 350; **3**.38, 40f, 155, 275–278; **4**.5, 13, 53, 143f, 146; **6**.48; **8**.16, 111f; **9**.13, 173; **10**.184; **11**.13, 77f, 108f, 166f, 196; **12**.56–60, 64–66; **13**.199f; **14**.131f, 252, 279, 346f; **15**.115f, 203; **16**.129, 152f; **17**.34, 39–41

constancy of **4**.221–223; **8**.166

Jewish **1**.80, 185, 191–198, 261f, 335; **2**.80; **3**.104, 135f; **4**.64, 223f; **7**.123; **10**.32f, 128, 184; **12**.95, 156f; **13**.47f; **14**.89f, 131f

laws of **6**.179–181

morning **6**.176

as sacrifice **17**.40f

Prayer-shawl **2**.287

Preaching **1**.75f, 79, 312, 352; **2**.69f, 108, 145; **3**.140, 245, 370; **4**.81, 134; **8**.137; **9**.39; **11**.53; **12**.31f; **14**.181f, 256, 307f, 336f, 347

apostles' **7**.22–24, 33–36; **9**.17, 25, 32; **14**.140f

defined **7**.67; **9**.176

equipment of 9.216f
gift of 9.111, 117f, 127–130
Greek 14.27–29
and healing 4.115f
Jewish 4.81, 160; 14.29f
the preacher 1.44f, 106, 285,
    385; 2.61, 91f, 289; 3.131f;
    9.24, 117f, 179, 208; 13.49;
    15.148
as proclamation 12.258
and virtue 12.52
Predestination 6.73; 8.114
Prefect 11.21
Prejudice 1.21, 50, 243, 338;
    2.60, 289; 3.127; 4.99, 124;
    5.193; 9.33, 192
Presbyters See Elders
Prestige 1.189, 285; 4.128;
    11.32
Pride 1.97, 137, 140; 2.14, 60,
    119, 288; 3.15, 128, 175,
    250, 330; 4.15f, 27, 135f,
    190, 223f; 5.193; 8.37, 53f,
    169; 9.34f, 38–40, 127, 182,
    197f, 232, 240, 244, 266;
    12.5, 73, 186f; 14.105f;
    15.58, 184; 17.80, 152–154
Priestesses 1.154
Priests 1.12; 2.211; 5.76f;
    6.104; 9.81; 12.109; 15.69;
    16.153; 17.34
  chief 1.29f; 2.261, 275, 374;
    3.346, 349; 4.243; 5.233f,
    253; 7.38; 14.263
Priesthood, Christian 12.1;
    14.199; 16.35, 178; 17.193
  Jewish 2.17, 217; 4.9, 275;
    5.77; 11.10; 13.45–47, 68,
    74, 78; 14.170

Principalities 8.117; 9.92; 10.92;
    11.96
Privilege 1.371, 383; 2.12, 61,
    108, 224, 263; 4.134, 151,
    245; 5.200; 6.186; 8.43, 52,
    173; 9.77, 122, 197; 10.124f;
    14.199; 15.72–74
Procurators 2.357
Profanity 12.37f
Profligacy 12.235
Progress, spiritual 13.50–55;
    14.299–307; 15.46, 77;
    17.105
Promise 1.48; 3.25; 8.126
  and fulfilment 9.176f
Promised Land, The 13.33, 35–
    37, 153f; 14.42, 173f
Property, Law of 4.204
Prophecy 1.5–6, 16, 36, 38, 43;
    2.8f; 3.17; 5.50, 157
  and fulfilment 5.115; 7.23,
    27, 105; 9.17; 10.96
  gift of 8.161; 9.111, 117f, 128
  interpretation of 14.311–314
  personified 1.52
  symbolism of 2.240–243, 253,
    341; 3.264, 270, 339; 4.239;
    7.154; 13.13
Prophetesses 16.105
Prophets 1.20, 80, 116; 2.5;
    3.16; 4.51, 245; 5.83, 145;
    8.12; 11.10; 12.227; 13.12–
    14; 14.180f, 293; 15.132–135,
    170; 16.25; 17.143, 171
  anointing 15.69
  clothing 1.282
  in Early Church 1.282; 4.134;
    7.91f, 98; 10.146f; 12.49,
    123; 14.79; 15.90; 16.12f;

| 1 Matt, v.1 | 3 Mark | 5 John, v.1 | 7 Acts | 9 Cor |
| 2 Matt, v.2 | 4 Luke | 6 John, v.2 | 8 Rom | 10 Gal, Eph |

17.127

false 1.281–288; 2.258; 3.49;
4.220; 5.77; 6.48; 7.91f;
10.147; 14.312, 314–318;
17.47, 130–132, 184

and the Law 1.127; 2.282

Promised one, the 4.115;
5.78; 6.72; 9.18

Propitiation 8.58

Proportion, sense of 2.293f;
4.188f; 10.90f; 12.253;
14.58, 77, 329

Proselytes 1.59f, 273; 2.290,
359; 3.14; 5.79, 126; 7.69,
106; 8.65; 9.106; 10.31,
111; 12.194, 262; 14.38,
79, 149; 16.80

Prosperity 1.181; 2.251; 3.246;
4.210f; 9.173; 12.185; 13.126

Prostitution 1.154, 156; 3.152;
9.52; 10.169f; 12.67; 17.137,
144

Proverbs, Book of 5.31

Providence 10.142; 13.15; 15.99

Proxenos, The 15.149

Prudence 1.256, 379; 2.47, 330;
9.215; 12.80, 239, 247, 251,
257

Pseudonymous Writings 14.30f,
32, 288

Psoriasis 3.44

Psycho-analysis 9.86

Ptolemais 1.40

Ptolemies 14.39

Publicans 1.329f; 3.53

Punishment 1.138, 175, 180,
386; 2.179, 182, 323; 3.228–
230; 4.214; 17.153

double 17.153

death-penalty 2.179, 357;
3.229; 6.233; 9.257; 16.90

everlasting 2.182

future 3.85f; 16.145

Jewish 3.113; 9.253

restorative 9.44–46, 182

Roman 2.179

and sin 2.98; 8.42

Purification 1.50f; 3.12, 234;
4.24f; 6.107; 14.246f

Purim, feast of 3.183; 9.228;
11.58

Puritans 2.372

Purity 1.119; 2.208; 3.236;
9.42, 174, 185, 215, 221;
11.19, 43, 80, 153f, 198–200;
12.99, 104; 13.102, 193;
14.61, 106–108; 15.75, 76–78;
17.105

of heart 1.51, 105–108; 2.16,
119; 9.193; 12.33f

symbolism of 16.122

Purple 14.221; 17.160

symbolism of 4.213

Purpose 1.177f; 5.35

Purses 1.367

Puteoli 7.190

Pythagoreans 8.182; 12.262;
13.197

Quakers 1.161; 2.52f

Quiet in the Land, The 4.26;
5.86

Quietness 17.143

Quiet Times 1.194; 3.123;
4.261, 298

Ra 3.71

Rabbis 1.86, 296f; 3.241, 279,

345; 4.94, 96, 115, 140, 253f,
275; 9.110, 251; 14.80
authority 1.134; 4.243f
disciples of 2.249; 4.273, 276
and Messiah 2.303
and sacrifice 13.199
sayings of 1.22, 52, 54, 56f,
110, 134, 139, 147, 151, 158,
159, 191, 236, 261, 268, 270,
304, 367, 379, 390, 393, 398;
2.18, 26, 48, 84, 144, 145,
188, 206, 225, 269, 303, 330;
3.17, 32, 47, 57, 104, 153,
231, 238; 4.10, 70, 118, 191,
209, 211, 216, 227, 253; 5.79,
83, 87, 97, 124, 126, 183, 213,
220, 243; 6.2; 8.70f, 187;
9.125, 136, 235; 10.168;
11.54; 12.76f, 129, 280f;
13.18, 47; 14.51, 69, 81, 85,
113, 127, 131, 134, 331, 347;
15.37, 45; 16.29, 48, 84, 95,
134; 17.221, 227
teaching of 2.236; 3.52, 85, 222,
260, 278, 331; 4.48, 81, 143,
230, 265; 8.55; 9.130; 10.27f,
40f; 13.67f; 14.132
titles of 2.287, 361; 3.32, 300
trade of 1.284, 366–368;
3.300; 4.254; 7.135; 9.79;
11.218
Racial memory 1.252
Rain 14.121
Rainbow 8.125
Ram, sign of 17.214
Ramadan 1.233
Ramah 1.38
Ransom 3.258; 8.59; 10.81;
16.34

Ranters, The 15.161f
Rapacity 8.34f; 9.53
Raphana 3.124
Readers 16.26
Reason 1.137; 10.131; 14.337
Rebirth See New Births, Renatus
Rebukes 12.102f
Received Text, The 15.111
Rechabites 12.119
Reciprocity, ethical 1.274;
2.160f; 14.222f
Reconciliation 2.189; 9.211;
10.67, 92, 117; 11.12, 122–
125; 13.187
word of 15.25
Red Sea 2.87
Redemption 3.217; 4.24; 5.133;
8.59; 9.57, 65, 152; 11.111,
115; 12.30; 13.104, 109;
15.99; 16.34; 17.31
Reed 2.5; 17.66
Reformation, spiritual 12.122
Reformation, The 1.357, 385;
3.61; 13.39; 14.77
Scottish 12.167
Reincarnation 8.182; 12.262;
14.88; 17.141
Religion 1.97, 107, 286–288,
323, 325, 354, 359; 2.4, 118f,
163, 166, 214, 278, 294, 296;
3.40, 64, 69, 122f, 168f, 214,
271; 4.8, 15, 156, 182; 8.50,
100; 9.46f; 10.10, 36f, 90,
151; 11.107; 13.1, 66, 77f,
102, 112, 138; 14.61f, 297,
304; 15.31, 39, 203; 17.110
duties of 1.187, 334f; 5.160
Jewish 1.128f, 185; 2.109,
115, 284–287; 3.165

---

and peace **13.**72
primary virtue **12.**134
way of **13.**74
and wisdom **14.**45
word of **15.**25
Rights **1.**167f
Rings **4.**205; **14.**64; **17.**23
Ritualism **1.**43; **11.**145
Roads **3.**17; **5.**79; **6.**138f
to the East **1.**40, 73
of the Sea **1.**39; **3.**52
from the South **4.**48
Robbery **9.**52, 53
Rock **2.**140; **5.**251; **12.**18
Rod **6.**55; **17.**66f
Roman Catholic Church **2.**139;
   3.61, 99; **6.**65
Romans, Letter to **8.**1–10;
   10.44; **16.**165
Rome **1.**113; **2.**135; **7.**89; **8.**1;
   14.159; **17.**63, 139, 164
army of **1.**300f; **6.**229; **8.**49
as 'Babylon' **14.**277f; **15.**19f;
   16.15; **17.**63, 134, 136, 149–
   151, 166–168
bishop of **2.**139; **12.**222
Church of **1.**120, 381f; **3.**209;
   8.1, 15, 207, 211; **9.**186;
   14.160
citizens of **7.**126, 163
colonies of **7.**123; **11.**3f, 30,
   69
doom of **17.**110f
emperor **1.**114; **3.**100
empire of **1.**25, 40; **3.**100,
   287; **7.**11; **12.**231; **16.**3,
   14–20, 36; **17.**88, 101
fear at **12.**190, 219
fever of **11.**49

fire of **12.**167
immorality of **8.**32
and Jews **9.**167; **11.**59
laws of **6.**252; **10.**86; **17.**219
luxury of **5.**212; **8.**31f;
   14.221; **17.**154–157, 158f
people of **3.**194
polytheism of **17.**138
prisoners of **7.**95
provinces of **3.**284; **9.**209f
as Restrainer **11.**213
riots of **7.**147, 169; **8.**30f
sayings of **1.**119
standard of **2.**358; **4.**280
Rust **1.**239; **14.**28

Sabbath **1.**126, 128, 286; **2.**19–
   23, 290, 374f; **3.**31, 39, 63f,
   67–69; **4.**70, 289, 291; **5.**6,
   30, 181f, 238, 241f; **7.**15;
   10.36; **16.**93; **17.**95
and circumcision **4.**24
and Gentiles **8.**48f
and Jesus **2.**26, 28; **4.**187;
   6.44f
journey on **3.**263; **4.**156
law of **1.**309f; **2.**21–27, 30f,
   208, 372; **3.**39; **4.**60, 177;
   5.121f; **8.**137, 180; **12.**264;
   14.69; **17.**19
meals **3.**37; **4.**187, 213
offerings **2.**24
rest of **17.**188
tyranny of **8.**184
Sabbatic years **10.**36f
Sacraments **2.**103, 296, 342;
   4.265, 295; **6.**262; **9.**42, 91–
   93, 110, 168; **12.**261; **13.**198;
   14.130, 245; **17.**34

---

1 Matt, v.1   3 Mark   5 John, v.1   7 Acts   9 Cor
2 Matt, v.2   4 Luke   6 John, v.2   8 Rom   10 Gal, Eph

Sacrifice
  and almsgiving 9.165
  Christian 1.115, 396; 2.87,
    151; 3.230f; 4.230; 8.58;
    10.25, 78, 117, 125, 161;
    11.16, 44, 46, 65, 86, 126;
    12.43f, 160, 208f; 13.151,
    195–199; 14.196f; 17.11, 31,
    108, 127
  heathen 9.71–76, 80, 91;
    13.197f
  Jewish 1.80, 119, 131, 142;
    2.245; 3.234; 5.112; 10.161;
    13.45, 78, 102, 113
  for proselytes 3.114
  Samaritan 5.157
  substitutionary 1.143
Sacrilege 13.125
Saddle, The 4.285
Sadducees 1.43, 355, 359;
    2.128f, 147, 211, 275–277,
    278; 3.288–291, 349; 4.249–
    251, 275; 5.86, 234, 249;
    6.93, 104, 113f; 7.37; 8.205;
    9.137; 16.84
  heresies of 14.316
Saffron 17.161
Sagan, The 4.273; 7.37
Saints 1.116, 354; 2.52; 7.77f;
    9.25; 10.150; 11.10; 12.45,
    83; 13.194; 15.4, 122, 176f;
    16.70
Salamis 7.97
Salt 1.85, 118–122; 3.234f;
    4.197f
  bond of 9.91
  and Christian life 3.233
  'of the covenant' 3.234
  at Passover 2.340; 3.333

Salvation 1.217; 3.25f, 213,
    226, 248, 256; 3.248; 4.220;
    5.7, 137, 190; 7.24; 8.13,
    19–21, 121, 134f; 9.39, 143;
    10.43; 11.40–44; 12.146;
    13.20f, 48; 14.174; 15.9,
    40, 100f; 17.28, 227
  chain of 1.398–400
  cost of 3.259; 6.161
  gift of 9.12; 10.56, 104;
    11.53
  and Gnostics 11.115f
  helmet of 10.183f
  the purpose of God 8.153;
    12.230; 14.180f
  universal 17.216
  wells of 5.249
  wholeness of 4.148; 7.178;
    10.163; 11.24f; 12.30f;
    14.175f
  word of 15.24
Salvation Army 3.54; 4.52;
    6.124; 9.208
Samaria 1.73; 2.95, 194; 4.31,
    129
  and Christianity 7.4f; 12.62f,
    64f, 88; 15.89
  and Dispersion 14.37
  and Pilate 2.359; 6.240
  Woman of 1.363; 5.5₂ 15,
    52f, 147–161; 9.132
Samaritans 1.363, 370; 4.5, 6,
    129, 139f, 217; 5.16; 7.4,
    62f, 64f; 14.37
  and Jews 5.6, 149, 157; 6.31
  Pentateuch of 5.159
Samos 7.150
Sanctification 2.202; 3.337;
    8.91

and justification **8**.77

Sandals **2**.367; **3**.17, 142; **4**.94, 285; **5**.98; **6**.139; **10**.183

symbolism of **4**.205

Sanhedrin **1**.12, 36, 140; **2**.258, 343; **3**.279, 312; **4**.247f, 275–277; **5**.123; **6**.103f, 260; **7**.38; **9**.186

administrators of **14**.263

apostles of **7**.177; **13**.30

composition of **2**.147, 353; **3**.346; **4**.133

and divorce **3**.239

local **3**.312

and orthodoxy **5**.77; **17**.131

police **3**.346; **7**.70

procedure of **4**.276; **7**.164

and Romans **3**.349; **7**.61

trials in **2**.353f; **3**.348f

Sanity **14**.251

Sapphire **17**.213, 215

Saracens **4**.111

Sard **17**.214

Sardian **16**.151f

Sardis **9**.89f; **12**.184; **16**.28, 113–115, 126; **17**.214

Letter to **16**.112–123

Sardonyx **17**.159, 213, 215

Saronic Gulf **9**.1

Saturn **1**.26

Saturnalia **17**.159

Scapegoat, The **13**.100f; **14**.244

Scarlet **17**.160

Sceptics, The **8**.159

Schism **14**.316

Schoenus **9**.2

Scoffers **1**.158

Scorpion **1**.271, 17, 51

Sign of **17**.215

Scourging **2**.363; **3**.358; **6**.244, 250; **7**.163; **9**.253f

Scribes **1**.29f, 128, 133f, 294, 328, 354; **2**.90f, 116, 165, 227, 280–282; **3**.31, 164, 279, 293, 299f, 346, 349; **4**.156f, 243, 275

Scribes and Pharisees **1**.6f, 8, 46f, 132, 286, 333f, 337, 355; **2**.16, 18f, 22f, 27, 30, 32, 35f, 44, 46, 50, 54, 109f, 113, 116–119, 121, 125, 147, 211, 280–284, 298, 323; **3**.56, 58, 76, 79, 165–167, 177; **4**.65, 91, 100, 161, 187f, 199; **5**.86, 122, 199; **6**.1f, 4f, 15, 165, 169; **14**.263; **15**.104

woes against **2**.288–299

Scripture **12**.198–202; **14**.337; **17**.34

and Jesus **2**.118; **15**.112

and Jews **1**.127; **10**.40f; **13**.67f; **16**.26

and Paul **8**.55; **9**.88f, 223; **10**.27f, **12**.177

Scruples **8**.180, 182, 194; **9**.73

Scythia **17**.159

Scythians **11**.155; **16**.97; **17**.194

Scythopolis **1**.81; **3**.124; **5**.147

Sea **2**.179; **9**.254; **17**.198

Seals **5**.145; **8**.87; **9**.78; **13**.14; **14**.244; **16**.166; **17**.1ff, 18, 21–23, 66, 99

Sealing **10**.87; **12**.177; **17**.23

Seasons **10**.36

Secret See Mystery

Sectarianism **2**.291; **12**.265

Secularism **4**.81

Security **5**.86f; **6**.59; **14**.228–

---

1 Matt, v.1	3 Mark	5 John, v.1	7 Acts	9 Cor
2 Matt, v.2	4 Luke	6 John, v.2	8 Rom	10 Gal, Eph

230; **16**.61; **17**.103
Seed **15**.78
Seemism **15**.7
Seleucia **7**.97; **14**.39
Seleucids **14**.39; **16**.87
Self-centredness **1**.202, 219, 396;
    3.335; **4**.164; **9**.22; **10**.48;
    12.236; **14**.329
  -control **1**.96f, 237; **2**.208;
    10.52, 138; **11**.67, 75, 85f;
    11.45; **12**.80, 144f, 239, 252;
    14.302f; **15**.188f
  -deception **1**.244; **4**.95; **15**.32–
  34
  -denial **2**.151, 173, 175, 182;
    3.232; **4**.121; **11**.150; **12**.161
  -esteem **1**.230; **2**.32, 325;
    3.112; **4**.190; **5**.193; **12**.180
  -examination **1**.244; **3**.175,
    261; **9**.249f; **10**.90, 135;
    13.1
  -pity **13**.178
Selfishness **1**.254, 323; **2**.103,
    205, 210, 219, 326; **3**.236;
    6.114; **7**.125; **9**.121f, 232;
    10.46; **11**.15, 23, 38; **12**.184,
    259; **14**.118–120, 227, 329;
    15.57, 190, 193f
  in marriage **2**.205
  in prayer **2**.190; **6**.180
  in worship **9**.130
Sensationalism **4**.44
Senselessness **8**.38
Sensualism **9**.52
Sephoris **4**.121
Septuagint, The See Index VI
Seraphim **8**.117; **13**.17; **16**.157f
Seraphs **16**.158
Serenity **1**.256; **10**.75; **14**.75,

272
Sermon on the Mount **1**.5, 9,
    33, *83–294*, 358, 372; **2**.206;
    476; **5**.160; **8**.6; **12**.201;
    14.22, 25, 126; **15**.83; **17**.153
Sermon on the Plain **4**.76
Serpent **8**.96; **16**.89f
  The Ancient **17**.80, 82, 98
  The Crooked **17**.58
Servant of the Lord **1**.310; **4**.38
Service **1**.97, 149, 169, 179, 225,
    248f, 308f, 310, 361, 392,
    400; **2**.25, 90, 186, 226, 230,
    232, 279, 323f; **3**.29, 38, 69,
    123, 203, 257f, 301; **4**.52,
    97, 118, 121f, 128, 132, 210,
    264, 267f; **5**.87, 142; **6**.124,
    136–140, 190, 217; **7**.78, 111;
    8.157, 159, 161, 202f; **9**.114,
    163; **10**.99, 124, 149; **11**.103,
    187; **12**.52, 148, 173; **13**.61;
    14.199, 255f, 293; **16**.25
Seven **1**.170; **5**.103; **7**.87; **8**.107;
    13.36; **16**.11, 28f, 172;
    17.117
  Spirits **16**.31f, 116, 155
Seven, The **7**.19, 52, 64
Seventy, The **4**.133, 135
Shadow and reality **11**.79;
    ˈ**13**.2f, 88
Shamelessness **3**.175; **8**.179
Sharon, plain of **3**.52
Sheba, Queen of **2**.50; **4**.151;
    14.42
Shechem **5**.6, 150
Sheep **2**.184; **6**.56
Sheepfolds **6**.58
Sheol **6**.91; **9**.137; **16**.9, 181;
    17.184

| **11** Phil, Col, Thes | **13** Heb | **15** John, Jude | **16** Rev, v.1 |
| **12** Tim, Tit, Phlm | **14** Jas, Pet | | **17** Rev, v.2 |

Hall of Hewn Stone **2.**353;
  3.349; **4.**276
Holy of holies **2.**243, 371;
  3.63, 365; **4.**288; **13.**62, 96;
  16.94; **17.**212, 221
Holy Place **2.**23, 243; **11.**10
inspectors of **5.**110
Mount of **1.**368
police **2.**335, 351; **5.**245;
  6.222
Royal Cloister **3.**278
Royal Porch **1.**68; **2.**305;
  3.308; **4.**44
profanation of **2.**241; **3.**267
sacrifices **1.**142f; **2.**26, 168;
  3.332f; **4.**10, 22f, 242; **5.**81
shewbread **2.**23, 244; **3.**63
of Solomon **5.**69; **16.**45;
  17.10, 203, 212
Solomon's Porch **1.**68; **2.**305;
  3.278; **4.**44; **5.**6
treasury **2.**168, 245; **6.**10, 70,
  239
Trumpets, The **3.**302; **4.**254;
  6.8
Water Gate **5.**249
veil of **2.**371; **3.**365; **4.**288
Temples, pagan **15.**124
Temptation **1.**199, 224–232,
  380; **2.**80, 180; **3.**130, 189;
  4.105f, 125, 144, 215, 270;
  8.221; **9.**76, 90; **10.**183;
  11.42, 71; **12.**251; **14.**42–44,
  50f; **15.**54f, 76, 106; **16.**119
avoidance of **9.**59, 257
laws of **6.**111
types of **9.**89f
Tempter, The **1.**64, 66; **2.**148;
  3.199; **17.**82

Ten **16.**79
Ten Commandments **1.**127, 130f,
  221; **2.**115, 214, 281, 285;
  3.31, 163; **4.**59f; **5.**69; **8.**52;
  9.190; **12.**38, 187; **13.**20;
  14.21, 60
Ten Tribes (lost) **5.**149; **14.**37;
  16.3
Tension **8.**199f
Tent of witness **17.**121
Testimony See Witness, Christian
Thanklessness **12.**187
Thanksgiving **4.**118; **10.**167;
  11.77f, 132; **12.**58
Theft **3.**173; **8.**39, 176; **9.**52
Theocracy **2.**272; **10.**108
Theology **1.**291, 342; **3.**29;
  5.56f; **9.**130, 161; **10.**45;
  11.108f; **12.**127; **14.**140;
  15.88; **17.**219
Theosophy **11.**99
Thermai **11.**180
Thessalonians, Letters to **11.**179–
  183
Thessalonica **2.**83; **4.**182; **7.**119,
  122, 127, 128; **11.**73; **12.**205
Thessaly **4.**31
Thirst **1.**99, 188
spiritual **5.**153; **17.**22
Thomist Church **6.**277
Thought **1.**136; **3.**124; **4.**150;
  11.210; **14.**77
Thousand **17.**192
Thrace **5.**178
Thracians **16.**97
Three **17.**117
Three Taverns **7.**190
Thrones **8.**117; **16.**148
Thyatira **16.**28, 66, 101f

Vigilance 1.65; 9.89f; 14.272
Villainy 8.34
Vineyard 4.245; 6.173f
  of God 2.261f
Violence 2.351; 12.122, 237;
  17.97
Virgin, sign of 17.215
Virginity 9.66f; 17.106
  Jewish 1.19; 2.196; 4.12
Virgin's fountain 6.43
Virtue 1.96, 278; 8.164; 9.40;
  11.157; 12.39, 61f; 13.46;
  14.300–305
  healing 1.308
Visions 1.243–247; 11.145f
Votive shields 6.239f
Vows 2.208; 7.166
Vulgate, the 6.291; 15.111

Wady Hamam 2.72
Wages 1.99; 2.245
Wailing 1.344; 3.134; 6.96f
  women 4.111
Wallet 3.142f
Wantonness 10.47, 153
Warfare, Christian 1.393;
  10.181–184; 12.159–160
Washings 2.114, 362; 3.13f
Watchers, The 14.322f; 16.175
Watchfulness 2.317; 4.260f;
  16.118f, 120
Water 1.188, 322; 2.340; 3.331;
  5.98, 129, 153f, 178, 249;
  17.125, 221
  living 5.152, 250; 17.220
Water-carrier 17.215
Way of the Sea 1.73, 330
Way of the South 1.39
Weak, The 2.80

Weakness 1.365
Wealth 1.239f, 249, 252; 3.244;
  4.165, 228f; 12.132, 137;
  13.62; 14.115f
Weddings, Jewish 1.19, 335;
  2.266, 319; 3.59; 4.66; 5.96f,
  143f; 9.246
Wells 4.188
Westminster Confession 1.53;
  5.56
Wheat 2.73; 9.80
Whisperers 8.36
White 16.98
  day 16.97
  horses 5.178; 17.167, 179
  ones 16.31
  robes 16.121–123; 17.26, 29f,
  121
  stone 16.95–97
  throne 17.194
Wickedness 3.174f
Widows 9.62; 12.3, 105f, 109–
  115
  Jewish 1.19; 4.12, 254; 12.105
Wilderness 1.63; 3.16, 23;
  4.43; 17.143
Wind 17.19f
Wine 1.391; 2.340; 3.333;
  5.97; 10.49; 12.79f; 17.6,
  162
  -presses 2.261f; 17.116
  -skins 1.338; 3.61
Wisdom 1.273; 2.10; 5.33;
  7.56f; 9.109; 10.82f; 11.108f,
  129; 14.93–97, 295
  gift of 14.45
  and Greeks 9.19; 15.79
  O.T. 11.117
  personified 1.52; 5.31

INDEX OF PERSONAL NAMES

Annas 3.274; 4.3, 32; 6.225
  bazaars of 2.246; 6.226
  booths of 4.242
Anthony, saint 1.149
Antisthenes 8.199; 9.37
Antiochus Epiphanes 2.28, 241,
    282, 306; 3.172, 267, 310;
    6.69; 8.137; 13.30, 166f,
    183; 14.202; 15.62f; 16.137;
    17.26, 60f, 62, 69, 79
Antiochus the Great 11.93; 14.40
Antiochus of Sardis 16.115
Antipas 16.92
Antipater 1.29, 36; 3.149
Antiphanes 12.35
Antistius Vetus 14.219
Antoinette, Marie 1.42
Anton, P. 12.2
Antoninus 3.85; 6.37
Antonia 12.200
Antony 7.168; 11.3; 12.78
Apelles 8.213
Aphrodite 1.154; 7.134; 9.3,
    52; 10.162; 12.38, 67; 16.75;
    17.144
Apicius 17.156
Apion 14.202
Apollo 1.289; 7.89; 10.34;
    15.124; 16.75, 89
Apollonius 2.80, 16.75
Apollos 7.138f; 8.209; 9.14f,
    36, 38f, 165; 11.103; 12.68,
    266; 13.9; 16.60
Apphia 12.277f
Apuleius 5.73, 127
Aquila and Priscilla 7.136, 139;
    8.7–9, 208–211; 9.5, 167f;
    11.172; 12.68, 221f; 13.9;
    16.60

Aquinas 2.119; 8.35; 9.174;
    12.2, 80
Archelaus 1.39; 2.95; 3.150,
    284; 4.31, 35, 237; 6.237;
    7.93; 14.38
Archelaus of Macedonia 9.260
Archippus 11.174; 12.159, 273,
    277f; 16.139
Aristarchus 7.181, 192; 9.229;
    11.169
Aristeas 1.134
Aristides 6.185f; 13.142, 192;
    15.85; 16.73f; 17.155
Aristion 5.23; 14.162f
Aristippus 14.84
Aristobulus 1.29, 36, 74; 3.149f;
    4.35f; 5.123; 7.93; 8.213
  household of 8.9
Aristophanes 13.191; 16.88;
    17.130
Aristotle 1.96, 302, 375; 2.246;
    3.246; 8.ix, 28, 36, 37, 45;
    9.40, 79, 109; 10.52, 82, 113,
    137, 179; 11.34, 158, 179;
    12.35, 39, 45, 61, 80, 83, 104,
    107, 186, 235, 236, 238, 240,
    259, 271; 13.174; 14.40, 58,
    84, 95, 186, 211, 300, 302;
    17.211
Armitage, A.H.N.G. 5.22, 100
Arnobius 8.172
Arnold, M. 1.216; 3.132, 235,
    251; 5.212; 9.123f, 198;
    11.79; 13.120; 14.96, 128;
    17.198
Artemas 12.265
Artemis 1.196; 7.140f, 146;
    12.89; 16.89
  Temple of 16.59

---

11 Phil, Col, Thes   13 Heb   15 John, Jude   16 Rev, v.1
12 Tim, Tit, Phlm   14 Jas, Pet   17 Rev, v.2

Artemon 8.ix
Arthur, King 2.372; 10.125
Asclepios 16.75, 91
 A. Soter 16.89
Asher, *Testament of* See Index VI
Ashmedai 6.31
Asidaeus 14.38
Asquith, C. 13.122
Asquith, M. 3.140, 144
Assael 3.34
Astor J. J. 1.348
Athanasius 13.5; 14.5; 16.161
Athenagoras 8.172; 13.12;
 14.280
Athene 10.174; 16.89, 91
Attalus II 16.125
Attalus III 14.145; 16.87
Augustine 1.133, 228f; 2.140;
 3.161, 294; 4.63, 193; 5.13,
 64, 86, 138, 155; 5.14; 6.81,
 290f; 8.96, 168, 177f, 190;
 9.18, 39, 192; 12.44, 263;
 13.8; 14.4, 207, 279, 323;
 15.6, 18, 41, 93; 16.119, 161;
 17.37, 130, 190f
Augustus, emperor 1.27, 29;
 3.71, 229; 4.31, 85, 237;
 5.98; 6.238; 7.123; 9.249;
 10.171, 180; 11.21, 137;
 12.78; 13.177; 16.17f, 99;
 17.89, 139, 146, 161
Aulus Fulvius 13.177
Aulus Plautius 12.223
Aurelius Archelaus 9.185
Aurora 1.271
Avery, M. 1.318; 5.209
Azai, rabbi ben 9.69, 256
Azariah 1.365
Azazel 14.322f

Bacchus 10.9
Bacon 6.242; 13.135
Bagehot, W. 12.204
Bailey, P. J. 12.171
Bain 1.348
Balaam 3.22; 14.332; 15.159,
 164, 190; 16.66f, 92; 17.81
Balak 14.333
Baldwin, S. 1.324; 3.223; 13.200
Ball, R. 15.162
Balthasar 1.31; 3.65
Barabbas 3.173, 356–358
 Jesus B. 2.361; 6.248f
Barachios 2.298
Barak 4.47; 13.163; 17.132
Barclay, F. 4.153
Bar-Jesus See Elymas
Barnabas 1.109; 3.3, 361; 7.19,
 75f, 90, 98f, 117f; 10.139,
 145; 12.44
 apostle 14.17
 Letter of See Index VI
 and Hebrews Epistle 13.8f
 and Paul 7.96–101, 117, 118;
 8.13; 10.19; 11.170; 12.21,
 217, 232; 17.110
Barrett, C. K. 6.166
Barrie, J. M. 1.41, 149, 229;
 2.250; 4.39, 168, 265; 8.64;
 9.121, 171; 11.72; 12.210;
 13.122, 138; 14.113, 273
Bartholemew 5.94f
Bartimaeus 3.260
Barton, B. 3.12f, 257; 4.267
Baruch
 Apocalypse of See Index VI
 Book of See Index VI
Basil 9.264, 265; 10.48, 135, 153
Basilides 12.8

Bathsheba 1.17; 3.85

Baxter, R. 15.161

Beare, F. W. 14.138, 142

Beatus 16.31

Becker 10.175

Beckwith 17.142

Bede 4.127

Beethoven 1.213; 7.189; 8.73, 166; 10.126; 13.117

Belden, A. D. 3.41

Belial 11.212; 17.59

Beliar See Belial

Belloc, H. 1.353

Benaiah 16.133

Bengel, J. 2.122f; 3.80, 174; 4.193; 6.126, 219; 8.59; 10.177; 11.13, 67, 163; 13.57; 14.220, 252, 300

Benjamin, *Testament of* See Index VI

Bennett, A. 4.137; 10.158

Bernanos, G. 5.233

Bernard, saint 16.147

Bernard, J. H. 5.74; 6.120; 10.135

Bernice 7.93, 174

Berokah of Chuza, rabbi 2.14

Beza 9.13; 12.173

Bias 14.55

Bigg, C. 14.143, 151, 176, 224, 230, 247, 300, 334, 348

Bilney, T. 4.91; 11.112; 13.56; 14.128

Binyon, L. 6.148

Birkett, N. 1.100; 3.153

Bishop, E. F. F. 1.121

Bithia 13.156

Black, J. 8.169

Blackie, J. S. 1.41

Blake, W. 2.373

Blastus 7.97

Boadicea, queen 17.5

Boanerges 5.16, 18

Boaz 6.146

Booth, W. 3.362; 4.68, 116; 9.208

Boreham F. W. 1.236; 4.8, 235; 8.124f; 10.89; 12.46

Borrow, G. H. 3.122

Boswell, J. 1.190; 3.152; 9.83, 160; 10.90

Botherich 12.205

Bottomley 15.161

Bradley, A. C. 1.244

Bridges, R. 1.223

Britannicus 17.91

Brooke A. E. 15.43, 47, 65, 77, 83, 97, 103, 115

Brooke, R. 1.115; 4.259f; 8.20

Brooks, C. 8.188

Brown, E. F. 11.103; 12.38, 40, 44, 55, 63, 80, 120, 129, 139, 193, 205, 248, 255

Brown, J. 1.285; 6.20; 7.18; 15.22

Brown, R. 1.227

Brown, R. McAfee 6.102

Brown, T. E. 3.186

Browne, T. 1.275; 14.92

Browning, E. B. 1.400; 3.186; 4.274; 5.142

Browning, R. 1.117, 214; 4.124; 5.155, 191; 6.32, 198f; 7.104; 8.20; 9.200, 202; 13.89, 178; 14.43, 247

Bruce, A. B. 3.5f; 4.195; 6.162; 9.179; 12.126; 13.70

Brugman 1.306

Cebes 1.278

Celsus 1.34, 289; 2.350; 5.73; 9.19, 21, 141; 10.122; 14.204
Against Celsus Sèe Index VI

Cephas See Peter, apostle

Cerinthus 5.12, 18, 21; 15.7f, 108, 144; 17.190

Cervantes 3.226

Cestius 2.328; 3.324; 4.263

Chalmers, J. 3.227; 4.35; 9.261; 13.22

Chamberlain, N. 3.140

Chanina, rabbi 1.390

Chapman, J. 1.244, 247

Charlemagne, emperor 4.111

Charles, R. H. 16.29, 89, 98, 103, 173; 17.40, 120, 123, 149, 172, 180, 232

Charlie, prince 9.92f

Charrington, F. W. 9.222

Chase, bishop 14.286

Chesterton, G. K. 1.14, 348; 3.264, 316; 4.44, 75, 77, 92, 96; 6.18; 8.181; 10.130; 12.171; 13.24; 14.349

Chija ben Abba, rabbi 1.327

Chillingworth, W. 10.90

Chirgwin, A. M. 3.82f; 6.94; 12.146, 199f

Chiyya, rabbi 3.86

Chloe ix.6, 8, 13

Chopin, F. 4.272

Christ See *Jesus*

Christie, W. M. 1.317

Chrysippus 2.313; 14.341

Chrysologus, P. 1.302; 14.211

Chrysostom 2.349; 3.3; 5.211; 6.49; 8.42, 168; 9.19, 20, 119, 212, 213, 218; 10.50, 116, 138, 167, 173; 12.11, 102, 256; 13.60, 152; 14.303, 324; 15.73; 17.113

Churchill, W. 1.132, 374, 380; 3.201; 5.28; 8.199

Chuza 4.96

Cicero 1.14, 139, 153; 2.164; 3.125; 6.250; 7.163; 10.82, 83, 113, 161; 12.78, 104; 13.2; 14.38, 99, 207, 303; 16.74, 138

Clark, A. 9.124

Clark, G. N. 10.85

Clarkson, T. 2.76

Claudia 12.222

Claudia Procula 2.359

Claudias Lysias 7.4, 167; 14.23, 36

Claudius, emperor 1.114, 344; 3.134, 320; 7.136; 8.7, 32, 106, 208f, 213; 12.222; 16.18, 59; 17.89, 90f, 93, 139, 144, 146

Clement of Alexandria, 1.160, 307, 379; 2.207; 5.10, 17, 21; 6.154; 8.28, 32; 9.109; 10.160; 12.249; 13.5, 7, 149; 14.10, 64, 134, 277, 280, 285; 15.19, 28f, 97; 16.67

Clement (N.T.) 11.74

Clement of Rome 9.214; 12.10, 60, 158; 13.161; 14.137, 141

Clementine
Letters of See Index VI
Recognitions of See Index VI

Cleopatra of Egypt 5.98; 7.168; 17.156

Cleopatra of Jerusalem 3.150

Clogg, F. B. 14.286

---

11 Phil, Col, Thes
12 Tim, Tit, Phlm

13 Heb
14 Jas, Pet

15 John, Jude

16 Rev, v.1
17 Rev, v.2

Clough, A. H. **2**.82; **4**.122; **12**.154

Clovis **9**.24

Cnaeus Domitius Ahenobarbus **17**.90

Cockburn, Lord **9**.188

Cogidubnus **12**.222

Coleridge, S. T. **1**.251, 280; **8**.178; **9**.85; **10**.62, 123, 157

Colman, R. **1**.262

Columella **8**.4

Confucius **1**.274; **4**.79

Conrad **7**.63

Constantine **1**.25, 120

Copernicus **1**.339; **3**.101

Coponius **6**.233

Cornelius Gallus **17**.51

Cornelius (N.T.) **1**.301; **2**.145; **7**.4, 5, 19, 79f, 88, 114; **14**.178; **15**.90

Cotton **9**.244

Courvoisier, Prof. **2**.31

Cousin, A. R. **11**.193

Cowley **3**.174

Cowper, W. **8**.166; **16**.65

Cranfield, C. E. B. **14**.169, 190, 195, 205f, 225, 227, 252

Cranmer, T. **1**.255

Crassus **5**.109

Crescens **12**.218

Crispus **9**.5, 16

Croesus **16**.113f

Cromwell, O. **1**.394; **3**.253; **4**.130; **7**.45, 53; **8**.183; **9**.34, 88; **10**.184; **13**.52, 165; **14**.340; **15**.145; **16**.91

Cromwell, T. **3**.329

Cronin, A. J. **4**.128

Crooks, W. **3**.138f

Curzon, Lord **3**.223

Cybele **9**.117; **10**.44; **12**.17; **16**.74f

Cynics **3**.127; **9**.37, 65

Cyprian **12**.59; **13**.5; **16**.84

Cyrenius **3**.285

Cyril of Alexandria **6**.283; **14**.323

Cyril of Jerusalem **6**.23; **9**.168; **14**.280

Cyrus **2**.33; **6**.5; **9**.89; **11**.92; **12**.186; **13**.60; **15**.36; **16**.114f; **17**.110, 128f

Dale, R. W. **1**.184

Damaris **7**.133

Damocles **14**.158

Dan, *Testament of* See Index VI

Daniel **1**.234; **13**.164

Dante **3**.156, 328

Daphne **7**.89

Darius **3**.202

Darwin, C. **4**.162; **6**.114

David, King **1**.9, 13, 47, 101, 225; **2**.23; **3**.22, 50, 63, 85, 193, 281; **4**.40, 70; **5**.82; **6**.142; **11**.10, 54; **13**.90, 163f; **14**.293; **15**.69; **16**.25, 133; **17**.59, 81

  city of **1**.24

  covenant of **13**.90

  house of **2**.145

  key of **2**.144; **16**.127

  kingdom of **17**.206

  line of **4**.26; **7**.23, 105; **16**.2

  servant of God **6**.178

Davidson, A. B. **10**.118

Davies, T. W. **9**.97

Davies, W. H. **7**.32; **12**.214

161; **6**.225

Edward I **7**.44

Edward the Confessor **6**.95

Edwards, T. C. **9**.167

Egnatius **14**.218

Eleazar **4**.214; **6**.105; **8**.137; **13**.168

Elektra **15**.19

Elgar, E. **14**.273

Eli **2**.42; **12**.134; **17**.59

Eliakim **2**.145; **7**.100; **16**.128, 133

Eliezer, rabbi **1**.56, 192, 194, 274; **2**.48f, 116; **10**.111

Eliezer ben Hyrcanus, rabbi **1**.34

Eliezer ben Jacob, rabbi **1**.368

Elijah **1**.44f, 49, 64, 282; **2**.14, 136f, 160, 287, 369; **3**.16, 22, 147, 211, 213, 364; **4**.19, 48, 90, 126; **5**.244; **6**.45; **8**.120, 144; **13**.164, 166; **14**.29, 132; **15**.69; **16**.6, 25; **17**.42, 79, 143

  meaning of name **4**.17

  at Passover **3**.338

  return of **2**.6, 164f; **3**.195f; **4**.115; **5**.78f; **17**.70f

  at Transfiguration **2**.156–63; **4**.123

Eliot G. **1**.247; **9**.150

Eliot, T. S. **6**.242

Eliphaz **3**.47; **4**.173; **6**.126; **10**.158

Elisha **1**.239; **2**.159, 287; **3**.24, 127; **4**.48, 86, 134; **13**.164, 166; **15**.69; **17**.42

Elizabeth **2**.96; **4**.4, 10f, 17

Ellicott, C. J. **11**.13

Elliott, W. H. **1**.312

El Shaddai **9**.188

Elymas **1**.26; **7**.19, 100; **12**.54

Emerson, R. W. **6**.244; **12**.34

Enoch **8**.104; **13**.133–135; **14**.238–240; **15**.159; **16**.122; **17**.70

  Book of See Index VI

  Book of the Secrets of See Index VI

  legends of **13**.134

Epaenetus **8**.8

Epaphroditus **7**.192; **9**.230; **11**.6f, 48–50, 74; **12**.159

Epaphras **11**.94, 107, 171; **12**.269; **16**.25

Ephraim **5**.152

Epicharmus **1**.278f

Epictetus **1**.274, 283, 336, 396; **3**.114; **4**.65, 278; **8**.19, 113, 197; **9**.55, 69, 140, 204, 254; **10**.13; **11**.85, 132; **12**.19, 58, 125, 159, 204, 265; **13**.62, 139; **14**.76, 207, 220, 304, 326; **15**.115

Epicurus **1**.55; **8**.19; **9**.22; **12**.129; **13**.129, 139, 195

Epidaurus **9**.110

Epimenides **7**.132; **12**.243

Epiphanius **13**.17

Erasmus **1**.385; **11**.124; **12**.208; **13**.57; **14**.277; **15**.111

Erastus **9**.21; **12**.222

Esau **4**.17; **8**.120, 128; **11**.58; **16**.133

  legends of **13**.183f

Esdras, *Apocalypse of* See Index VI

Eudemus **12**.236

Eumenes **16**.88

Eunice 11.47; 12.68
Euodia 11.71–74; 12.68
Euripides 8.202; 9.140, 155;
   10.25, 48; 12.80, 107f, 236,
   239; 13.111, 132; 14.95,
   298; 17.4
Eusebius 1.81; 2.360; 4.112;
   5.3, 17, 18, 23; 12.11, 61,
   118; 13.5; 14.5, 12, 151,
   204, 285; 15.7, 38, 127, 167;
   16.14; 17.79, 141, 190, 231
Euthymius Zigabenus 6.290
Eutychus 7.149
Evans, C. 6.124
Evans, E. 1.312
Evans, M. 1.247
Eve See *Adam & Eve*
Evelyn 1.37
Ezekiel 14.79
Ezra 1.12, 74; 2.281; 4.40;
   5.150; 7.65
   Apocalypse of See Index VI

Faber 1.341; 4.6; 11.83; 13.162
Fabiola 2.80
Falconer, R. 12.144, 158, 164,
   235
Farmer, H. H. 5.112
Farrar, F. W. 9.2, 4; 14.147
Farson, N. 1.294
Faustus 6.83
Felicitas 14.211
Felix 3.312; 7.94, 166–168, 171;
   12.283
Festus 3.312; 7.4; 172–176,
   178; 11.188; 14.12
Findlay, J. A. 2.319; 3.62; 5.192
Fisher, H. A. L. 10.85
Fisher, Lord 14.82

Flaccus 11.93; 16.139
Flavius Clemens 8.216; 9.21
Flavius Sabinus 8.217
Fleming, A. L. 14.128
Foch, Marshal 4.53; 12.160
Foligras, Andela di 3.123
Forbes, R. 8.72
Fortunatus 9.6, 8, 166
Fosdick, H. E. 1.288; 3.42;
   4.68; 6.129; 7.101; 9.120;
   12.218; 13.130; 16.65
Foster, J. 7.10; 13.43
Fowler, W. 12.61; 14.304
Fox, G. 1.161, 396; 15.145, 161,
   162
Foxe, J. 4.151; 9.214
Francis of Assisi 2.326; 3.24;
   4.95; 6.138; 10.56; 12.254f
Francis of Sales 2.107
Frankau, G. 1.262; 6.87
Frazer, J. G. 5.178
Freeman, K. J. 2.80
Freud, S. 9.86
Friedlander, L. 14.202; 17.154
Frohman, C. 13.138
Froude, J. A. 5.58; 6.112;
   8.26; 9.147; 14.340; 17.86
Fry, E. 3.107

Gabriel 10.93f; 13.18, 156;
   14.323, 325; 16.31, 174;
   17.41, 175
Gaius 15.131f, 135, 147f, 150
Gaius of Augustus 3.229; 15.37
   of Corinth 8.220; 9.16; 15.148
   of Derbe 15.147
   of Macedonia 15.147
   of Rome 1.302; 10.180
Galba, emperor 3.257; 8.130;

11 Phil, Col, Thes
12 Tim, Tit, Phlm
13 Heb
14 Jas, Pet
15 John, Jude
16 Rev, v.1
17 Rev, v.2

16.19; **17.**89, 92f, 139
Galen 3.146; **12.**176; **13.**82,
   193; **14.**129; **16.**89
Galerius **12.**59
Galileo 3.101f; **4.**68
Gallio **7.**3f, 137; **9.**5; **16.**15
Galloway **6.**93
Galsworthy, J. **3.**28
Gamaliel **7.**49f, 160; **11.**59
Gamaliel II, rabbi **6.**89
Gandhi **2.**254
Garfield, president **1.**231
Garibaldi, G. **1.**375; 3.201;
   6.191
Gee, H. L. **1.**399; 2.62f; **6.**206;
   9.172, 261; **10.**129
Gehazi **1.**239
George V **6.**275; **9.**172
Gibbon, E. **3.**205; **4.**85; **8.**173
Gibbs, P. **3.**108; **6.**242; **10.**91,
   113
Gideon **4.**47; **13.**163; **17.**180
Gilbert, H. **7.**184
Gilbert, W. S. **13.**136
Gladstone, W. E. **4.**148
Glaucus **12.**151
Glover, R. **2.**143, 145, 175
Glover, T. R. **1.**323, 394, 397;
   4.130; **5.**73; **6.**138; **7.**128;
   8.15, 185; **11.**85; **15.**41
Godet, F. L. **5.**91; **6.**100
Goethe, W. **1.**75; **5.**48; **8.**181
Gog **17.**60, 194
Goldsmith **10.**90
Goodspeed, E. J. **3.**287; **5.**7, 26;
   10.68; **11.**126; **12.**269, 274;
   14.30, 138; **15.**7; **16.**16
Goodwin, T. **12.**46
Gore, C. **9.**145

Gorgias **12.**156
Gorion **5.**123
Gosse, E. **3.**122
Gossip, A. J. **4.**8; **6.**162; **10.**13;
   12.160; **13.**45, 72
Gough, J. B. **10.**54
Graham, Billy **3.**13
Gray, T. **1.**279
Green, B. **7.**72
Gregory the Great **2.**235; **3.**258
Gregory of Nazianzen **13.**82
Gregory of Nyssa **2.**234; **3.**258;
   8.16; **12.**127
Grenfell, W. **1.**135; **5.**105, 191,
   236f; **7.**175
Grenville, G. **2.**76
Grice, S. Le **1.**220
Gunkel, H. **17.**133
Gunther, J. **10.**11

Haarhoff, T. J. **10.**123
Hadrian **1.**25; **9.**54; **13.**87
Hagar **8.**128; **10.**41; **11.**58
Hamilton, W. **6.**162
Hananiah **2.**240; **3.**339
Handel **6.**195; **9.**195; **16.**151
Hankey, D. **6.**140; **8.**15; **14.**337
Hannah **4.**15; **14.**112; **17.**59
Hannibal **13.**126f
Hanum **16.**143
Hanway, J. **1.**339; **6.**185
Hardy, H. E. **1.**208
Hardy, T. **1.**215; **3.**344; **4.**189;
   5.219; **8.**15; **10.**91
Harnack, A. **3.**33; **10.**69; **13.**9,
   193
Harris, R. **14.**238; **15.**130
Harrison, P. N. **12.**155
Hastings, J. **9.**97

| 1 Matt, v.1 | 3 Mark | 5 John, v.1 | 7 Acts | 9 Cor |
| 2 Matt, v.2 | 4 Luke | 6 John, v.2 | 8 Rom | 10 Gal, Eph |

Hawkins 1.190
Hazael 15.69
Healy, G. 1.16
Heawood, G. 1.353
Hegesippus 14.10, 12, 14
Heine 1.204; 8.43
Heli 4.41
Heliodorus 12.149
Helofernes 13.164
Helvidius 14.20
Henley 8.74
Henry V 1.126; 7.111; 9.216
Henry VI 12.176
Henry VIII 1.386; 3.206; 4.186
Henry, O. 3.230; 4.15; 6.109;
   16.64
Heracles 17.103
Heraclitus 3.57; 5.34f; 15.124;
   16.60
Herbert, G. 1.41, 183; 9.65;
   12.123, 128
Hercules 12.26
Hermas, *Shepherd of* See Index VI
Hermes 5.222; 7.109
Hermogenes 12.156; 17.140
Herod Agrippa I 2.97, 135;
   3.256; 7.93, 96f; 14.9
Herod Agrippa II 7.93
Herod Antipas 1.39, 71, 331;
   2.1, 93–98, 133, 136; 3.53,
   146, 150, 160, 187f, 213, 237,
   284; 4.3, 31, 35f, 115, 186,
   222, 237, 278–280; 6.237;
   7.93
Herod the Great 1.12, 28–30,
   36–39, 43; 2.95, 134; 3.53,
   149–153, 284; 4.31, 35f, 237;
   5.116, 237; 7.93, 167; 12.78
Herod Philip 2.94, 97; 3.150,

191; 4.3, 31, 35, 173, 237;
   6.237; 7.93
Herodias 2.94–96; 3.149f, 152f;
   4.35f; 7.93
Herodion 8.213
Herodotus 1.365; 4.7; 6.119;
   9.154; 11.92, 180; 12.17,
   151; 13.48; 14.261; 17.103,
   128
Histories of See Index VI
Hervey, H. 12.216
Hesiod 1.278; 5.178; 10.82
Heywood, T. 16.75
Hezekiah 5.134; 6.43; 12.150;
   13.164, 166; 16.128; 17.22
Hieronymus See Jerome
Hilarion 2.81
Hilary of Poitiers 14.3
Hillel, rabbi 1.170, 263, 273,
   284, 367, 390; 2.198, 200;
   3.113, 164, 239, 293; 4.79;
   6.70; 10.169
  school of 1.152; 4.212
Hind, L. 3.51
Hippocrates 12.280; 16.89
Hippolytus 14.312; 15.70;
   16.67; 17.25, 85
Canons of See Index VI
Hitler, A. 5.234; 15.63; 17.100
Hogan 9.244
Holland 3.181
Holmes, O. Wendell 1.120
Homer 3.138, 335; 5.98; 9.167;
   10.109; 12.234; 13.110, 117;
   14.216; 16.73, 75
Honorius 3.204
Hood, T. 9.203
Horace 1.279; 9.155; 12.78,
   245; 17.156

---

11 Phil, Col, Thes   13 Heb   15 John, Jude   16 Rev, v.1
12 Tim, Tit, Phlm   14 Jas, Pet   17 Rev, v.2

the Bridegroom **1.**336; **5.**143

burial of **2.**371f; **3.**365f;
   4.289f; **6.**262–4

carpenter **1.**41f, 59; **2.**17;
   3.6, 76, 138, 193, 254; **4.**37,
   237; **5.**123, 174, 219, 236,
   239; **6.**20, 107, 160, 222;
   11.218

centrality of **1.**79; **5.**82; **9.**130;
   14.337; **15.**22, 93, 178;
   17.180

and children **2.**174–181, 211f;
   3.7, 224, 241; **4.**127, 225–227

Christ, The **2.**137f; **3.**196;
   5.88; **8.**86; **10.**32, 132;
   11.11, 15, 32, 67, 104, 131f,
   148f, 152f; **15.**13f

commission of **2.**378

compassion of **1.**297f, 354f;
   2.15–18, 99; **3.**6f, 182f;
   4.86, 117; **5.**9; **6.**39; **11.**18

courage of **2.**19f, 242, 350;
   3.252, 268, 283, 335, 351;
   4.107, 230, 239f; **5.**187, 236,
   243; **6.**108, 119, 126, 223,
   244

courtesy of **4.**295

and creation **5.**40f; **6.**18;
   11.95, 114, 119f; **13.**15, 31;
   14.185; **16.**140f

cross of **1.**32f, 60f, 65, 70, 104,
   337; **2.**18, 33, 99, 120, 136,
   147–149, 156f, 161f, 211, 227f,
   230, 326, 343; **3.**60, 192, 210–
   212, 215f, 220, 241, 251, 282,
   327, 340, 343f, 350f; **4.**67,
   119f, 127, 196, 230f; 282–
   289, 297f; **5.**135; **6.**19f, 101,
   171, 204; **7.**26; **9.**33; **10.**25,

26f, 114; **12.**9; **13.**58f;
   14.185f; **15.**107

crucifixion of **2.**363–370; **3.**8,
   360–365; **4.**153, 288, 297f;
   5.2, 5, 13, 134f; **6.**234, 245,
   292; **7.**33f; **9.**15; **15.**8

day of **9.**12; **15.**118

death of **3.**362f; **4.**287f; **5.**135,
   251; **6.**67, 261; **8.**93; **9.**17,
   202, 209; **11.**122f, 142;
   14.185, 242; **15.**109; **16.**177f;
   17.30–34

deity of **2.**135, 206; **3.**6; **4.**51,
   138; **5.**14f, 39, 52, 74, 148,
   183, 188; **6.**68f, 74f, 161,
   215, 217f; **7.**25; **9.**151;
   11.34–37, 39, 70, 95, 115;
   13.4, 14, 19, 31, 44, 119;
   14.154, 294; **16.**110, 127,
   180; **17.**138

deliverer **9.**23

and Hades **14.**232, 236–243;
   16.52

disciples of **2.**77f, 120f, 125f,
   133, 212, 224, 229, 249, 304,
   333, 377; **3.**27–29, 38, 74,
   83, 155, 218, 252f; **4.**267f,
   274, 292; **5.**5, 16, 85–95;
   6.190, 213f; **7.**15

the Door **6.**58f

emotions of **3.**6f

eternal **6.**36; **16.**49; **17.**226

exaltation of **13.**15, 84, 86f,
   117f; **14.**141, 185

example of **4.**293; **11.**34f;
   13.173; **14.**214

exodus of **2.**160, 162

expiation of **15.**14f, 39f; **17.**31

faithful **17.**178

family of 2.229; 4.102; 5.231
233; 6.83, 257; 7.15, 95;
14.9f, 14–20; 15.171
fasting of 1.234, 325
feeding of five thousand 2.98–
103, 125f; 3.1f, 7; 5.4, 10,
10, 200–208
finality of 2.130; 11.95, 116–
118; 16.23
the Firstborn 11.119, 121;
16.32
the First-fruits 9.149–151
the Forerunner 6.155; 13.63
forgiveness of 2.345; 3.49–
52; 6.203, 231
the Foundation 2.140; 9.32
friendship of 1.369; 2.10;
3.26; 6.177
fullness of 5.71; 11.118f
and the future 2.300
in Galilee 2.126f; 3.41, 70,
73, 237, 262f; 4.45; 5.2, 4,
91, 106, 141
genealogies of 1.8–9, 11–13,
14–15; 3.298; 4.3, 12, 40f;
7.23; 13.74, 161
generosity 14.297
and Gentiles 3.177–179
gentleness of 9.238
in Gethsemane 1.65; 2.148,
191, 256, 343, 348, 350f; 3.8,
343, 347f; 4.271f; 5.1, 89,
126, 221; 9.199; 13.47, 74;
14.272; 17.97
glorification of 6.81, 123, 204
glory of 2.162; 3.211; 5.9,
14, 68–70; 6.81, 148f, 219f;
11.210; 13.14f, 86f; 16.150,
180

'Lord of glory' 1.25; 8.197
goodness of 8.81
gospel of 8.221; 12.149
grace of 7.142; 8.199; 9.144,
169; 10.143; 12.44, 48;
17.232
greatness of 3.190; 5.226;
6.152, 195; 14.296–298
healings of 1.80, 83, 354;
3.39, 119, 131f; 4.177f, 187
the Herald 1.352f, 362
the High Priest 6.254; 13.4,
31, 41–48, 70f, 79, 80–82,
119f; 15.93; 16.45f
and history 4.137f; 8.222;
12.230; 15.93
holiness of 13.83; 16.127
honesty of 1.111, 374, 393f;
2.231, 310; 3.201, 250; 4.131,
259; 6.154
honour of 16.180
our hope 12.19–21
hour of 3.70; 4.37, 45; 5.102,
231; 6.78, 81
humanity of 2.314; 3.6f; 4.41,
50, 138; 5.14, 65, 147f, 223;
6.50, 258, 261f; 8.103;
11.34–37, 95, 98, 115, 118;
12.90, 164; 13.4, 31, 44, 84;
15.9, 14, 23f, 93f, 143, 180
humility of 6.137; 11.6, 38
image of God 11.116–119
incarnation of 1.104; 3.80,
139; 4.23, 40, 274; 5.13, 14,
63–70; 6.148; 8.14, 157, 222;
9.18f, 141, 157; 10.144f;
11.36f; 12.90, 127, 256f;
13.103f, 15.6–9, 14, 23f, 61,
93, 105, 142f; 16.22, 63, 160;

17.58, 62
influence of **2**.6; **6**.164
and Jerusalem **2**.158f, 160,
  299; **3**.262f; **4**.124, 186;
  5.2f, 106f; **6**.101
of Judah **13**.70, 79; **16**.169,
  172
the Judge **2**.316; **3**.51; **5**.9,
  189f; **6**.15, 20, 246; **7**.14, 132;
  9.206f; **12**.202; **13**.111;
  14.22, 141, 195; **15**.176;
  16.146; **17**.194f
justice of **14**.294
and the keys **2**.144; **16**.48
kindness of **2**.127, 231
kingship of **1**.9, 32f, 40, 115,
  371; **2**.104, 137, 239, 242f,
  361; **3**:15, 27, 144, 160, 256f,
  265; **4**.26, 169, 238–240, 247,
  278; **5**.43, 50, 80; **6**.116, 130,
  241f, 243, 246f, 252; **9**.107;
  10.141; **11**.39, 111; **12**.136,
  203; **13**.15, 110, 118; **14**.122,
  347; **15**.93; **16**.32, 46, 146;
  17.183
knowledge of **11**.63–65;
  14.178f
'Lamb of God' **4**.23, **5**.80–82,
  153; **14**.185; **15**.77
the Lamb **16**.27, 157, 168–
  172; **17**.30, 83, 96, 98, 102,
  107f, 112, 118, 141f, 147,
  172f, 208
language of **1**.88, 314; **6**.271
and the Law **1**.9, 126–133,
  298; **2**.118; **4**.72; **10**.114f
law of **10**.78; **14**.21
legends of **4**.286
liberator **1**.13; **2**.341

life of **1**.40–43; **2**.11; **3**.1f,
  5f, 139f; **4**.1, 134, 185f; **5**.75,
  106f; **6**.279; **7**.9, 10; **9**.24,
  130
life-giver **5**.43, 189; **6**.60, 158;
  15.15, 100
the Light **1**.122–125; **5**.9, 10,
  45; **6**.10f, 13, 64; **6**.85;
  10.164f; **13**.56; **16**.53
limitlessness of **5**.72
loneliness of **3**.7, 251; **6**.202
lordship of **1**.114; **2**.123, 234,
  312, 342; **4**.261; **6**.183;
  7.14, 26; **8**.11, 139; **9**.11,
  107; **10**.141; **11**.9, 39, 70–72,
  122, 132; **12**.91, 136f;
  13.118; **14**.21, 184f; **15**.24,
  68; **16**.16, 33, 169; **17**.89,
  183
love of **1**.293f; **6**.149f; **9**.125,
  144; **10**.9, 132f; **11**.18, 56;
  16.33
loveliness of **2**.211f; **3**.80, 191
made sin **2**.369; **3**.19f, 364
majesty of **6**.243; **9**.184;
  16.172
master **2**.239; **4**.3; **5**.76
mediator **12**.29, 62f; **13**.15,
  89; **17**.176
meekness of **16**.172
mercy of **15**.54
merits of **9**.13
messiahship of **2**.353; **3**.264f,
  350; **4**.239; **5**.154, 161f, 185f,
  192; **6**.72, 118; **14**.24; **15**.6,
  68, 93, 107, 110; **16**.170
miracles of **1**.308f; **2**.101f;
  3.37f; **5**.9, 52, 119, 232
mission of **1**.72, 80; **4**.14

sufferings of 2.147, 227, 348f;
363f; 3.342; 4.271f, 275f;
5.14; 6.244, 246f; 11.64;
12.168f; 13.26f, 47; 14.258,
286, 311; 15.14; 16.131f
sufficiency of 10.65f; 11.134f;
12.241
supremacy of 5.12, 92, 142,
144; 13.14, 16, 31, 33
our surety 13.31
sword of 16.93f
sympathy of 2.344; 4.87;
5.149; 6.96–99, 203; 13.27f,
42f
and the synagogue 2.53f;
3.29–32
the Teacher 1.311, 353;
2.339; 3.31, 84, 138; 5.152
teaching of 1.4, 8, 83–87;
2.1, 54, 273; 3.32f, 144;
5.2, 20–23; 14.25, 60
and the Temple 2.20, 243–
248; 5.2, 4, 107, 114–117;
6.101; 10.51
temptations of 1.61–70, 83,
224f, 358; 2.36, 148, 171,
252; 3.6, 21–24, 160, 199;
4.41–44; 5.1, 80, 204;
6.161; 13.42; 16.33; 17.82,
143
transfiguration of 2.156–163;
3.209–211; 4.123f; 5.4;
16.51
trial of 2.343, 352–362, 373;
3.354f; 4.275f, 277–281;
5.53; 6.233–249; 12.136
the Truth 5.66f; 13.13;
14.316; 17.178
touchstone of truth 2.42, 129;

15.143
unifier 10.66
uniqueness of 5.165; 6.66;
8.139; 11.95, 115, 134;
12.31, 153; 13.33, 87, 101;
14.233; 15.13, 68, 163, 165,
180; 16.23, 32
victory of 2.220, 228, 312,
369f; 4.288; 6.258; 8.21;
9.183; 11.87, 142f; 13.118;
14.242f; 15.77f, 106; 16.178;
17.3f, 66, 167f, 177–183
the Vine 5.9; 6.172–176; 9.80
voice of 17.229
the Way 5.46; 9.17; 13.82
wisdom of 2.308; 5.242;
9.22; 16.179
the witness 16.32
woes of 2.288–299
work of 2.3; 3.23; 5.52, 104;
6.205f, 209–211; 7.82f; 8.23,
103; 10.101–104, 122–125;
11.143; 14.231–243; 15.35–
40, 112; 16.33–35; 17.17,
31f
worship of 1.30, 297f; 2.123
yoke of 2.17f
Jesus Barabbas 2.361f
Jesus ben Sirach 14.45, 63, 82,
113
Book of See Index VI
Wisdom of See Index VI
Jesus called Joshua 7.100
Jesus called Justus 11.170
Jezebel (O.T.) 1.64, 152; 2.198;
3.175, 239; 4.48; 9.266;
10.47; 16.105
Jezebel of Thyatira 16.66, 102–
110

Joab **16**.133

Joachim **13**.18

Joad, C. M. **4**.175; **11**.151

Joan of Arc **4**.14; **6**.124, 133, 204f; **9**.199; **12**.221

Joanna **4**.96

Joash **2**.298

Job **14**.29, 35, 125; **16**.25

Jochanan, rabbi **1**.368, 387f; **2**.182; **5**.150; **13**.103, 199

Jochebed **13**.155

John, apostle **1**.77; **2**.228, 230f; **3**.54, 253; **4**.127, 129, 265; **5**.15–18; **6**.266f; **7**.1, 32, 38; **8**.221; **14**.162; **16**.134; **17**.148

 Acts of See Index VI

 beloved disciple **3**.329; **5**.19; **6**.145

 legends of **5**.96; **10**.94

 name of **4**.17

 religion of **13**.1

 the un-named disciple **6**.228

John, Augustus **1**.348, 371

John the Baptist **1**.7, 43–60, 71; **2**.1–7, 10, 92–98, 99, 136, 258; **3**.11–20, 30, 146, 150f, 154, 213, 279; **4**.31–36, 89f, 115, 244; **5**.141–146, 245; **6**.25, 163; **9**.261; **14**.72; **15**.23, 109; **17**.143

 baptism of **4**.37; **5**.79f, 84; **6**.79; **7**.139, 141

 birth of **4**.8–11, 14, 16–19

 death of **7**.93

 disciples of **1**.78; **2**.2; **4**.5; **7**.141f

 emergence of **4**.3; **5**.2f

 in John's Gospel **5**.49f, 70f,

141

 prayers of **4**.143

 preaching of **3**.20f; **4**.6; **5**.45; **7**.141f

 sect of **5**.11f, 50

 witness of **5**.75–82, 85, 195f; **15**.112

John of Damascus **14**.4

John the Divine **16**.11–13

John the Elder **5**.23f; **14**.162; **15**.128

Johnson, L. **1**.350

Johnson, S. **1**.190, 242, 268; **2**.218; **3**.39, 247, 361; **4**.134, 156, 191; **5**.206; **9**.83f, 160; **10**.155; **11**.154; **12**.171, 216; **13**.73; **14**.336; **17**.198

Johohanan **4**.17

Jonadab **12**.119

Jonah **2**.49; **4**.151

 and Jesus **2**.20

 sign of **2**.129

Jonathan **16**.46

Jones, S. **4**.15

Jose ben Chalafta, rabbi **13**.29

Jose ben Jehuda, rabbi **2**.193

Joseph of Arimathea **2**.219, 372–374; **3**.263, 366f; **4**.289f; **6**.263

Joseph, husband of Mary **1**.8, 18f, 33f, 39, 41; **3**.65, 139; **4**.12f, 21, 29f, 41; **5**.96; **14**.17–19

Joseph (O.T.) **1**.15f, 39, 93; **4**.40; **5**.147; **7**.56f; **13**.153f; **14**.31; **15**.37; **16**.143; **17**.23

 Life of See Index VI

Josephus **1**.12, 27, 37, 45, 72, 77, 161, 295f, 359; **2**.28f,

6.90, 227

Malchus 2.351

Maltby, F. R. 4.77; 10.124

Malthake 3.150; 4.35

Manaen 7.98

Manasseh 1.58; 3.231; 5.150, 152; 9.221; 13.166

Manasses 13.164

Manoah 10.129; 13.3, 192

Marcion 10.68; 12.3, 139; 15.144; 17.106

Marcus 12.192

Marcus Antonius 12.39

Marcus Aurelius 1.154; 3.11, 25; 4.285; 5.58, 64; 10.170; 13.87, 111, 139

Marduk 11.212; 15.61; 17.58, 77, 133, 198

Mariamne the Boethusian 3.150; 4.35

Mariamne the Hasmonaean 1.29, 36; 3.149; 4.35; 7.93f

Mark, John 3.3f, 72, 347f; 7.97, 101f, 192; 10.39; 11.169f; 12.217f; 14.278

Marlow, N. 1.339

Marlowe, C. 6.83

Martha 1.104; 2.329; 3.263; 4.4, 141f; 6.80, 91, 96f, 109–111; 15.138

Martial 1.157; 8.4, 204; 10.171; 12.222; 14.187

Martin, H. 2.77, 225

Martin, J. 1.v

Martin, K. 11.200

Martin of Tours 11.326

Martineau 12.204

Marvell, A. 4.171; 8.177

Matthias 16.133

Mary, queen 2.194; 9.180

Mary of Orange 2.320; 11.205

Mary Tudor 12.52

Mary of Bethany 1.104; 2.329; 3.263; 4.4, 141f; 6.80, 91, 96f, 109–111

Mary, wife of Clopas 2.229; 6.255; 14.16

Mary, mother of James & Joses 2.374; 5.96–98; 14.16

Mary, mother of Jesus 1.18–20, 33, 41; 2.79, 96, 373; 3.139; 4.4, 5, 12–16, 21, 29f, 39, 41, 181; 5.19, 101f; 6.28, 82f, 255–257; 11.136; 12.68; 13.11f; 14.17, 19f; 15.138

Mary Magdalene 2.229, 376; 4.4, 96; 5.19, 48; 6.256, 264–267; 12.68; 14.16

Mary, mother of Mark 3.3, 347; 7.95; 12.217

Mary, the other 2.376

Mary (Rome) 8.214

Masterman, E. W. G. 1.295; 3.43

Mathathias 13.170

Matheson, G. 9.124; 10.103

Matthew, apostle 1.4–5, 329–332, 359; 2.189; 3.53–57, 74, 83; 4.64, 75, 82; 5.3, 23, 94; 11.136; 14.8, 162

Maugham, S. 2.205; 14.223

Maurice, F. D. 6.175

du Maurier 10.97

Maurois, A. 1.380; 10.85, 155

Maximus of Egypt 4.21

Maximus of Tyre 12.51

Maxwell, W. D. 1.195

Mayor, J. B. 14.46, 47, 134,

---

11 Phil, Col, Thes
12 Tim, Tit, Phlm
13 Heb
14 Jas, Pet
15 John, Jude
16 Rev, v.1
17 Rev, v.2

3.21f, 132, 211, 281; **4.**133;
5.52, 134, 215, 237–239, 241;
6.27, 45, 54f; **9.**88, 189–192;
10.27; **11.**10, 187; **12.**70,
134, 177, 194, 227; **13.**3, 31,
33, 89, 154–159; **14.**35, 181,
262, 292; **16.**25, 123; **17.**70f,
98, 143, 152, 196, 200
Ascension of See Index VI
Assumption of See Index VI
body of **15.**158, 166
and the Law **1.**366; **2.**160f;
3.293; **5.**72; **8.**118, 123;
10.6, 29f; **16.**24, 161
law of **2.**16, 281; **4.**250; **5.**5;
7.21; **8.**81; **10.**6; **13.**17,
185f
legends of **7.**58; **9.**125; **13.**18,
155, 156, 201f
pre-existence of **17.**96
and Samaria **2.**359; **5.**157
seat of **1.**7
servant of God **6.**177; **8.**12
Song of **17.**117–120
at Transfiguration **2.**159f,
163; **4.**123
uniqueness of **13.**28f
veneration of **1.**187
Moule, C. F. D. **11.**106, 108,
110, 150, 152, 165, 168
Muír, E. **1.**220
Muirhead, L. **6.**162
Muller, M. **11.**155
Muratori **5.**21; **14.**152
Muratorian Canon See Index VI
Muretus **4.**16; **14.**47
Murray, A. V. **3.**215
Murray, G. **12.**20, 80; **16.**159
Mussolini **15.**63

Myers, F. W. H. 3.í32, 191;
8.124; **9.**254; **15.**121, 122;
16.52

Naaman **1.**239; **3.**127; **4.**5;
5.187; **14.**112, 116
Nabal **17.**59
Naboth **4.**47
Nain, widow of **4.**4; **5.**9; **6.**100;
16.168
Nannacus **7.**107
Naphtali, *Testament of* See
Index VI
Napoleon **1.**39; **2.**138; **5.**211,
235; **6.**5f; **7.**109; **9.**121;
13.159; **15.**28, 63; **17.**100,
132
Narcissus **8.**9, 213
Nathan **3.**50, 85, 89
Nathanael **2.**252; **5.**91–95;
16.150
Nebuchadnezzar **8.**166; **13.**129,
164; **14.**39; **17.**77
Necho **17.**132
Nehemiah **1.**74, 230; **2.**168,
281; **4.**40; **5.**150; **6.**117;
7.65
Nelson, Lord **1.**32; **4.**265; **7.**30;
8.169; **10.**48; **12.**88
Nelson, J. **11.**52
Nemeseis **16.**75
Nepos **17.**190
Nereus **8.**9, 216f
Nero **1.**27, 112; **2.**135, 328;
3.324; **4.**263; **6.**183; **7.**167;
8.4, 106f, 172f, 204, 213;
9.21, 53f; **10.**121f; **11.**128;
12.11, 18, 59, 78, 166f, 211;
13.6, 58, 130; **14.**10, 138,

8.100, 221; 9.14f, 36, 143f;
10.17, 18–20, 102; 14.145,
162, 292, 347f; 16.134;
17.108
Acts of See Index VI
character of 2.106f
Chief Apostle 14.262
confession of 2.137–139;
3.180, 192f; 5.230; 14.195
courage of 2.351; 14.154f;
17.97
denial of Jesus 3.351–353;
6.227–231; 14.90, 268;
15.119
faith of 2.140f
and Gnosticism 11.136
Gospel of See Index VI
house of 3.39
and James 4.16; 14.10
and John 4.16
in John's Gospel 6.101, 141
and the keys 2.139–146
legends of 3.145; 10.93; 13.58
and Mark 3.72
and Paul 10.17, 18–20;
14.347f
preaching of 2.345; 3.4f, 7–8,
157; 7.5, 24–29, 33f
rebuked 1.65, 225; 2.51, 148–
150; 3.174, 199; 5.4
religion of 13.1
wife of 14.277
wife's mother 1.307f; 3.36–38
Peter Lombard 3.258
Peter Pan 1.149f; 9.160; 13.51,
138
Petronius 17.157
Phaniel 13.18
Pharaoh 8.120, 131; 12.194

Philemon 1.173; 11.164, 169;
12.270, 273, 274, 278, 283
Philemon the Greek 14.46
Philetus 12.174, 178
Philip, apostle 1.39; 5.5, 15, 16,
23, 52, 91, 94, 202, 204f;
6.120, 159, 163; 7.62;
14.162; 17.107
Philip, evangelist 7.4, 19, 62,
64f, 69, 88; 12.68; 15.89;
16.105
Philip II 9.120
Philip of Macedon 2.84; 7.122f;
11.3, 180
Philip of Neri 13.173
Philip, Tetrarch 2.95, 133, 135;
3.53, 150
Phillips, J. B. 16.118
Philo 1.134; 2.358, 364; 3.196;
4.79; 5.36, 64, 83, 183;
6.237, 247; 8.96; 10.99;
11.117, 159; 12.39, 80, 107,
131; 13.2, 12, 52, 80, 91, 134;
14.55, 60, 84, 98, 126, 323;
15.37, 190; 16.70
Philodemus 3.125; 12.236
Philostratus 9.19; 12.124, 125
Phineas 11.60
Phocylides 12.131
Phoebe 8.7, 207; 9.186
Phygelus 12.156
Pilate 1.8; 2.353, 357–363, 377;
3.354; 4.3, 31, 153, 172f,
277–281; 6.231–249; 13.130
Acts of See Index VI
bodyguard 2.363
character of 6.237–240
shade of 2.362
wife of 2.359

| 1 Matt, v.1 | 3 Mark | 5 John, v.1 | 7 Acts | 9 Cor |
| 2 Matt, v.2 | 4 Luke | 6 John, v.2 | 8 Rom | 10 Gal, Eph |

Pindar 8.46

Pitt, W. 2.76; 12.98

Pius 1.377

Pizarro 1.374f; 6.191

Plato 1.27, 136, 173, 279; 2.203, 313; 3.17, 113, 174; 4.36, 124; 5.8, 73, 140; 6.38, 168; 7.63; 8.167; 9.35, 51, 53, 79, 140, 186; 10.52, 83, 90, 113, 153, 183; 12.80, 81, 98, 107, 109, 207; 13.1, 2, 39, 88, 191; 14.99, 114, 186, 203, 217, 288, 316, 337, 341; 15.41, 42, 123, 149; 16.151; 17.199, 211

Definitions of See Index VI

Plautius 9.21

Plautus 1.385

Pliny 1.378, 398; 5.212; 6.42, 189; 8.36, 49; 9.21, 107; 10.179; 11.159; 12.67, 78, 99, 270; 13.193; 14.128, 155f, 161, 221; 16.97, 137; 17.155, 158f, 160, 213, 214

Letters of See Index VI

Plotinus 9.204

Plummer 1.73, 311, 359, 374; 2.14, 46, 288; 15.107, 118, 121

Plutarch 1.119; 3.202; 5.64, 8.45; 9.18, 19, 40, 71; 10.51, 83, 99, 156; 12.62, 124, 182, 185, 237; 13.43, 46, 207; 14.295, 302; 16.21; 17.103

Pluto 14.346

Pole 9.120

Polybius 1.301; 4.84; 12.237, 242, 258

Polycarp 1.115; 5.20; 9.107, 171; 11.7, 15; 12.19, 169; 14.137, 141f, 162; 15.9, 144; 16.76

Polycrates 6.228

Pompey 2.28; 3.68, 125; 5.123; 12.78; 14.38

Pomponia 12.223

Pomponia Graecina 9.21

Pomponius Mela 8.4

Pope 3.129

Popilius Laena 13.30, 167

Poppaea Sabina 6.183; 12.78, 14.149; 17.91

Potter, G. 2.24

Pouyanne 2.31

Praxiteles 7.141

Premanand 2.99, 101, 111, 211, 291; 11.103

Prescott 1.375

Primasius 17.142

Prisca See Aquila and Prisca

Priscilla See Aquila and Prisca

Priscillian 15.110

Prometheus 1.200

Propertius 8.31; 12.78

Prudentius 17.33

Psammetichus 14.39

Ptolemy 1.155; 16.88; 17.179

Ptolemy Lagos 2.29

Publius 7.188f

Publius Sempronius Sophus 14.219

Pudens & Claudia 12.222

Pusey 1.294; 4.106

Pythagoras 2.47; 8.112; 9.26; 10.99, 156; 12.80; 13.52, 62, 196; 16.21

Pytho 7.124

G

Samson 10.129; 13.163; 14.115f

Samuel 1.234; 2.276, 296; 4.17; 5.82; 6.126; 12.134; 15.69

Samuel, Viscount 1.340

Sanballat 5.150

Sanday, W. 1.65; 8.1

Saphira See Ananias & S.

Sarah 8.128; 10.41; 14.222

Sariel 17.41

Satan 1.65; 2.36f, 40, 51, 148–150, 317; 3.22f, 78f, 174, 330; 4.150, 263, 270, 273f; 6.31, 126; 8.34, 219; 9.181f, 195f, 246; 10.182; 11.193; 12.91, 93; 14.50; 17.47, 59, 80–84, 86, 88, 130, 168, 184, 190, 191f

and death 16.141

delivery to 9.44; 12.53f; 15.118

depths of 16.108f

power of 11.112, 212

prosecuting angel 13.18

seat of 16.88–90

synagogue of 16.80

Saturninus 12.94

Saul, king 2.276; 4.17, 47; 11.54, 58; 15.69; 16.46, 133

Saul of Tarsus See Paul

Schopenhauer 3.25; 5.231

Schürer 2.303; 3.194

Schweitzer, A. 9.83

Scipio 12.18

Scott, E. F. 5.160; 10.66, 67, 68; 12.217; 13.5; 14.283

Scott, R. 4.126; 11.72

Scott, W. 4.19; 8.74; 9.219; 13.83

Scythinus 3.57

Seago, E. 5.112

Seeley, J. 6.3; 14.229; 15.204

Selwyn, E. G. 14.143, 178, 190, 257

Semjaza 14.322

Seneca 1.27, 32, 139, 157, 283, 344; 3.12, 25; 4.26, 181; 5.55, 58; 6.23; 7.137; 8.4, 19, 31f, 39, 98, 204; 9.54, 140, 204, 235, 254; 10.81, 171, 176; 11.199; 12.19, 34, 51, 78, 130, 131, 159, 231, 245; 13.139, 157; 14.60, 64, 82, 113, 207, 221, 335: 15.100, 121; 16.117, 159; 17.91f, 145, 161

Epistles of See Index VI

Serapis 1.111; 3.181; 9.72

Sergius Paulus 7.3, 100; 9.21

Seth (Greek) 2.65; 3.91

Seth (O.T.) 14.323

Sennacherib 6.43; 17.22

Severus, A. 14.129

Shackleton 1.375

Shadrach 1.117; 8.166; 9.119; 13.129, 164

Shaftesbury, Lord 1.94, 166; 10.155

Shakespeare, W. 1.117, 244; 2.225, 297; 3.19, 206, 329; 5.224; 6.51; 8.33; 10.64, 82; 12.128, 189; 13.117, 135, 136, 137; 14.92, 266, 329; 17.28

Shammai, rabbi 1.273; 2.198, 200; 3.164; 6.70; 10.168

school of 1.152, 158; 3.239; 4.212

Shaw, G. B. 3.28; 4.11; 5.58; 6.129; 7.75; 8.40

14.42; 15.87; 16.3; 17.81, 206

and Jesus 2.20

Odes of See Index VI

Psalms of See Index VI

temple of 2.161

Solomon, pianist 9.244

Solon 1.154; 10.162; 12.38, 106; 16.114

ben Soma 9.256

Sopater 8.220

Sophocles 1.173; 8.202; 9.136, 158; 10.25, 110; 14.172, 298

Sosipater 8.220

Sosthenes 11.103

Spence 5.142f

Spenser 12.209; 17.114

Sporus 17.91

Spurgeon, C. H. 5.100, 163; 12.204

Spurius Carvilius Ruga 1.156; 8.32; 10.171

Stalin, J. 4.114

Stalker 9.7

Stanley 7.12

Stanton 6.204; 9.120

Starbuck, E. D. 6.40f

Statius Quadratus 9.107

Statilla Messalina 12.78

Stephanas 9.15f, 166

Stephanatus 9.6, 8

Stephanus 3.299; 9.223; 15.111

Stephen 4.285; 6.86, 233; 7.4, 5, 19, 53f; 14.259

defence of 7.54–61

and Paul 7.74f

prayer of 7.62, 72; 8.168

Stevenson, R. L. 1.100, 121,

222f; 3.153, 245; 4.66, 106, 167; 5.55; 8.22, 64, 91, 177; 9.196, 203, 235f; 10.182; 13.120, 150; 14.92; 15.55; 16.82

Stewart, H. F. 14.92

Stewart, J. 9.24

Stilicho 3.204

Stoddart, J. 1.276

Stowe, H. B. 9.188

Strabo 11.91; 14.40; 16.58, 74, 87, 126; 17.45, 166

Strachan, R. H. 6.87

Stradivari, A. 7.45

Strahan 16.41

Streeter, B. H. 14.151, 163

Struma Nonius 14.221

Struthers, J. P. 1.285; 3.327; 7.31; 13.151

Studd, C. T. 3.58; 12.56

Sulla 12.78

Suetonius 1.27; 3.181, 229, 313; 6.182; 8.31; 10.171; 14.157; 17.139f, 154, 156

Suidas 14.107

Sullivan, A. 10.123

Sulpicius Gallus 14.218

Sulpicius Severus 14.149

Sunday, B. 3.12

Sutherland, H. 12.213

Swedenborg, E. 1.305

Swete, H. B. 3.80; 16.33, 38, 50, 51, 121, 151, 154, 156, 159, 169, 172; 17.17, 26, 41, 77, 79, 83, 93f, 110, 117, 120, 130, 131, 132, 133, 151, 171, 172, 176, 177, 180, 190, 192, 197, 209, 219, 221, 224, 225, 227, 229

Swinburne **1.**120, 213; **4.**195; **8.**72; **13.**135

Symeon (Peter) **14.**291f

Syntyche **11.**71–74; **12.**68

Tabitha **5.**90; **6.**87; **7.**77

Tacitus **1.**27; **2.**218, 364; **3.**313, 320; **6.**41f, 182, 250; **7.**168; **8.**31, 49, 50; **12.**20, 36, 78, 167, 190; **13.**111, 178; **14.**147, 149, 202; **15.**124; **16.**138; **17.**83, 145, 146, 154, 160
Histories of See Index VI

Tagore **10.**8

Tamar **1.**17

Tarphon **1.**367

Tatian **12.**59; **14.**152; **17.**106

Tatlock, R. **11.**33

Tauler **1.**260f

Taylor, Fr. **10.**113

Taylor, J. **3.**122, 174; **8.**36; **12.**80; **13.**27

Taylor, V. **10.**45; **15.**143

Telemachus **2.**77; **3.**203–205

Temple W. **2.**117; **3.**89

Tennyson, A. **1.**227; **2.**321; **3.**200, 226; **4.**226, 276; **13.**1, 20, 27; **14.**132

Terah **13.**143

Tertius **8.**xii, 45, 220; **11.**174

Tertullian **1.**111, 267; **2.**349, 360; **3.**13, 317; **8.**27, 172; **9.**63, 222, 258; **12.**1, 59, 64, 170; **13.**5, 8, 149, 192; **14.**20, 129, 279, 280; **15.**70, 169; **16.**26, 70, 92; **17.**12, 70, 141, 189
and Scripture **14.**3, 151

Tertullus **7.**168f

Thackeray **9.**219

Thaddeus **1.**82

Thalasius **2.**80

Thecla, *Acts of Paul* See Index VI

Theocritus **11.**203

Theodore of Mopseuestia **2.**349; **12.**116f, 204

Theodoret **1.**266; **2.**349; **8.**34f; **11.**124

Theodorus **3.**125

Theodosius **12.**159, 205

Theodota **1.**155

Theognis **10.**110

Theophilus (N.T.) **4.**1, 3; **7.**2, 9; **12.**11

Theophilus of Antioch **12.**59

Theophorus **2.**175

Theophrastus **8.**37, 38; **12.**186; **13.**191; **14.**105, 265; **15.**58, 197

Theophylact **8.**37; **12.**186; **13.**182; **14.**105

Theresa, saint **8.**71

Thermouthis **13.**156

Theudas **1.**69; **7.**50; **9.**18

Thomas, apostle **5.**5, 23, 90; **6.**87f, 101, 156f, 270, 275–279; **14.**161, 162, 179, 294
Acts of See Index VI
called Didymus **7.**100

Thomas à Kempis **15.**87

Thompson, F. **6.**160; **8.**153; **9.**199

Thomson, W. M. **1.**77, 316, 322, 344; **2.**21, 72f, 76, 84, 134, 253; **6.**57, 61, 281

Thorwaldson **2.**249; **9.**92

Thurio **12.**127

1 Matt, v.1	**3** Mark	**5** John, v.1	**7** Acts	**9** Cor
2 Matt, v.2	**4** Luke	**6** John, v.2	**8** Rom	**10** Gal, Eph

Thucydides 9.3, 155; **14**.82, 108, 143

Tiamat **11**.212; **15**.61; **17**.58, 133, 198

Tiberius **2**.359; **3**.125, 286; **4**.3, 31; **6**.239; **8**.31; **10**.171; **11**.21, 137; **16**.18, 75, 115, 126, 135; **17**.89, 93, 139, 146, 160

Tiberius Claudius Cogidubnus **12**.222

Timothy **3**.4, 71; **7**.120, 136; **8**.219; **9**.5, 6, 8, 41, 165; **11**.47f, 74, 103f, 181, 195; **12**.21–23, 49, 50, 51f, 96, 98, 133f, 138, 164f, 197; **15**.171

Tiridates **1**.27

Titus (Emperor) **2**.302, 306; **9**.183; **16**.19; **17**.89, 93, 101, 139, 146

Titus (N.T.) **9**.7, 8, 183, 224–226; **10**.16; **12**.71, 218f, 232

Tobias **1**.273

Tobit, *Book of* See Index VI

Tolstoi **4**.40; **9**.188

Toplady **6**.262

Torpacion **14**.129

Toscanini **1**.135; **3**.17; **4**.51; **10**.126

Tournier, P. **1**.327; **2**.31; **3**.35, 37f, 47; **6**.5; **13**.60

Trajan **1**.391; **6**.189; **9**.21, 107; **11**.159; **12**.99; **13**.193; **14**.128, 155f, 159

Trench, R. C. **8**.42; **9**.170; **10**.51, 136; **11**.157; **12**.37, 61, 80, 83, 236, 239, 240; **14**.330; **16**.60, 63, 133, 140, 141, 144, 145, 148

Tristram, C. **1**.345; **2**.157, 251; **5**.153, 212f

Trophimus **7**.157; **10**.112; **12**.222

Tryphaena and Tryphosa **8**.214

Trypho, *Dialogue with* See Index VI

Tsze-Kung **1**.274

Tullia **12**.78

Tulloch, Mrs **1**.105

Turgeniev **9**.262

Turner, C. H. **7**.4

Twitchell, J. **9**.132f

Tychicus **7**.192; **10**.61f, 185; **11**.169; **12**.219, 265

Tyndale, W. **1**.255; **3**.180; **4**.152; **6**.189; **8**.167; **12**.220

Tyrimnus **16**.101

Tyrranus **7**.142f

Tyrrell **5**.51

Ulysses **3**.336; **8**.186; **9**.52

Unamuno **4**.182; **10**.124; **17**.118

Urban VIII **3**.101f

Uriah **1**.17; **3**.85

Uriel **13**.18; **14**.325; **16**.31; **17**.41

Valentine **12**.127

Valentinus **12**.8

Valerius Maximus **17**.156

Varro **1**.302; **10**.179; **14**.211

Varus **1**.395

Vaughan, C. J. **8**.55, 96; **13**.14

Vedius, P. **10**.180; **12**.270

Verrall, A. W. **1**.153

Verrius Flaccus **9**.249

Verus **1**.154; **10**.170

11 Phil, Col, Thes
12 Tim, Tit, Phlm
13 Heb
14 Jas, Pet
15 John, Jude
16 Rev, v.1
17 Rev, v.2

INDEX OF FOREIGN WORDS, TERMS AND PHRASES

Amachos 12.84, 259
Amarantos 14.174
Amemptos 11.43, 60
Amen 9.177; 16.37, 140
Ameth 5.213
Ametor 13.74f
Amiantos 13.84; 14.173
Amixia 8.50
Amnos 16.171
Amomos 10.78; 11.44; 15.207;
  17.108, 161
Amphiblestron 1.77; 2.88f;
  3.27
Anagke 9.213
Anakainosis 8.158
Analuein 11.28
Analusis 12.209
Anamartetos 6.4
Anapempein 12.274, 281
Anastrephesthai 12.88
Anastrophe 14.201
Anathema 8.124
Andrapododes 10.135
Androphonoi 12.38
Andropodistai 12.39
Aneleemon 8.39
Anemeros 12.190
Anepileptos 12.75
Anhupotaktoi 12.37
'Ani 1.91
Anoche 8.42
Anomia 1.221; 3.357
Anomoi 12.37
Anosios 12.37, 188
Anothen 5.125
Antallagma 2.154
Anthropos 6.244
Anti 15.61
Antilutron 16.177

Antistrategos 15.61
Antitheseis 12.139
Antitupos 14.244
Anupokritos 14.97
Aorgesia 1.96
Apagoge 1.144
Aparabatos 13.82
Aparche 17.108
Apatheia 6.98; 9.18; 13.42;
  14.75f
Apator 13.74f
Apatouria 10.34
Apaugasma 13.14
Apechein 1.186
Apecho 1.186
Apeitheia 8.38
Aphanismos 13.92
Aphilagathos 12.190
Aphorozein 8.12
Aphrosune 3.175
Aphthartos 14.173
Apo 11.26; 16.21
Apokalupsis 3.305; 14.122;
  16.2, 21
Apokaradokia 8.110f; 11.26
Apokatallassein 10.117
Apokruphos 11.130, 148
Apokruptein 11.148
Apollyon 17.51f
Apologia 11.17
Apolutrosis 8.59; 10.81
Apostellein 5.165; 10.74; 12.17;
  15.176
Aposthesthai 14.189
Apostolos 4.74; 7.177; 10.74f;
  11.49f, 103; 12.17, 148; 13.30;
  15.176
Aproskopos 11.19
Aptaistos 15.206

Arbel 17.50
Arbiter bibendi 5.99
Arbitri 13.89
Arche 11.121; 16.141; 17.204f
Archegos 13.25f
Archetheoria 8.202
Architriklinos 5.99
Archomenoi 13.52
Archon 5.123
Areskeia 12.62
Areskos 12.236
Arete 11.81; 14.301f
Argurion 2.332
Ariston 16.147
Arles 9.177
Arnion 16.171
Arnoumai 17.101
Arnoume 17.101
Arrabon 9.177, 205; 10.87
Arsenokoitai 12.38
Artemisia 17.44
Asebeis 12.37
Asebes 12.37
Aselgeia 3.174f; 8.179; 9.265f;
    10.47, 153; 14.319; 15.180
Aselgese 15.180
Asher 4.56
Ashere 1.88
-Asmos 8.91
Asotia 12.234
Asotos 12.235
Aspondos 12.188
Assarion 1.389; 4.171
Asthenein 1.365
Asthenes 1.365
Astorgos 8.39; 12.188
Astrateia 8.49
Asunetos 8.38
Asunthetos 8.38f

Ataktein 11.217
Ataktos 11.217
Ataraxia 8.199
Atheotes 8.49
Athetesis 13.79
Athlein nominos 12.161
Atimia 9.217
Augustus 17.138
Autarkeia 9.235; 11.84; 12.128
Autarkes 11.84
Authadeia 12.62, 236
Authades 12.236; 14.329f
Autodiakonos 1.90
Autos 14.329
Ayont 9.203; 13.150
Azazel 13.100

Baptizein 3.255; 4.169; 5.84
Barbaroi 7.187; 13.148
Basileia 16.40
Basilikos 5.174
Bastazein 6.112; 8.197
Bath 5.98
Bath qol 3.20; 6.127
Bdelugma 12.246
Bdeluktos 12.246
Be 16.34
Bebaiosis 11.17
Bebaptismenos 3.255
Bebelos 12.37f; 13.182
Bela 16.66
Bema 9.206
Beneficiarius 9.185
Biblia 12.219
Biblos 1.12
Blasphemia 1.324; 3.175;
    11.153; 12.187
Brekekekex coax coax 17.130
Brosis 1.239

11 Phil, Col, Thes	13 Heb	15 John, Jude	16 Rev, v.1
12 Tim, Tit, Phlm	14 Jas, Pet		17 Rev, v.2

Didaktikos **12**.82
Didaskalos **1**.311; **5**.87
Didrachma **2**.168; **4**.172
Diekrithete **14**.65
Dikaios **8**.23; **9**.79f; **12**.239; **13**.142
Dikaiosune **8**.23, 34; **10**.164; **11**.62; **12**.134
Dikaioun **8**.22, 57
Dilogos **12**.85
Diolkos **9**.1
Diorussein **1**.239
Dipsuchos **14**.46
Dispensator **14**.255
Dives **4**.213
Divus **17**.89, 138
Dokein **5**.13, 65; **11**.26; **15**.7, 180
Dokimazein **11**.18
Dokime **8**.74
Dokimion **14**.43
Dokimos **12**.173; **14**.48
Dolos **3**.174; **8**.35f; **14**.190
Doloun **8**.36
Domina **15**.138
Dominus **17**.89, 138
Dorcas **7**.77
Douleuein **1**.248
Doulikos **10**.135
Douloprepes **10**.135
Doulos **1**.248; **6**.177f; **8**.11f; **11**.9; **12**.227; **14**.35f, 210, 292, 293; **15**.175; **16**.24f
Doxai **14**.323
Drachma **2**.168, 222; **4**.172, 202
Dunamis **5**.119; **7**.180
Dusnoetos **14**.349
DWD **1**.9

Ebedh **16**.25
Ebion **1**.91
Ecclesia haeres crucis est **12**.169
Echein **14**.318
Echthroi **8**.152
Egguos **13**.81
Egkomboma **14**.270
Egkombousthai **14**.270
Egkoptein **11**.193
Egkrateia **10**.52; **14**.302f
Egkrates **12**.239
Eikon **11**.116–118; **13**.112f
Eikonion **11**.118
Eile **11**.19
Eilein **11**.19
Eilikrineia **9**.174, 185
Eilikrenes **11**.19; **14**.337
Eilikrines dianoia **14**.337
Eimi **16**.30
Eirein **11**.12
Eirene **10**.9, 50, 76; **11**.12; **14**.95, 97
Eirenikos **14**.95
Ek **15**.92
Ekbasis **9**.90
Ekklesia **2**.142; **12**.88f; **14**.21, 26
Eklektos **14**.167
Ektenes **14**.252
Ekzetesis **12**.5
Electrum **16**.49
Eleemon **1**.103
Eleemosune **9**.164
Elegchein **6**.192; **12**.239; **16**.144
Elegchos **16**.145
Elekte **15**.19, 129f, 138
Elekte kuria **15**.129f, 138
Eleos **12**.24; **14**.96
Eleutheria **12**.9

Frail 3.184
Fugitivus 10.180; 12.122, 270

Galil 1.72; 4.45
Gallicinium 2.347; 3.352; 6.230
Gan 4.56
Gazam 17.50
Geneseos 1.12
Genomenos 16.30, 81
Genus Boswellia 17.162
Geraskon 13.92
Geron 12.280
Gerousia 12.70
Gignesthai 11.37
Gignomai 16.30
Ginoskein 11.63
Gnesios 12.22f
Gnosis 9.109, 130; 12.139;
    14.294, 302; 15.10
Goggusmos 5.237; 11.43
Goggustes 15.197
Graphein 6.3
Gumnasiarcha 8.202
Gumnos 13.40
Gunai 5.98
Gunaika 16.104
Gune 16.104

Ha'am 16.66
Hadon 14.329
Hadrotes 9.163f
Haggadah 3.338
Hagiasmos 8.91; 13.181f
Hagios 15.4, 176; 16.93, 127;
    17.152
Hagiazo 9.10
Hagiazein 6.77, 216
Hagiazesthai 1.205
Hagios 1.205; 6.77, 216; 7.78;

8.94; 9.10; 10.77, 108; 11.10;
    13.181; 14.188, 199
Hagnos 11.80; 14.95
Hagnotes 9.215
Hairein 12.265
Haireisthai 14.316
Hairesis 10.48; 14.316
Hairetikos 12.265
Halal 17.169
Hallel 2.342; 3.338; 5.249;
    6.116; 17.169
Hallelujah 17.168f
Halusis 11.21f
Hamartia 1.220; 6.17; 10.95f;
    14.233; 15.33
Hamartolos 3.56f; 12.37;
    14.107
Hanukkah 6.69
Haplos 1.245
Haplotes 1.245; 8.161f
Haplous 1.245; 8.162
Hargol 17.50
Harpagmos 11.36
Harparchein 11.35
Harpax 9.53
Hasil 17.50
Hathos 8.118
Hedraioma 12.89
Helkuein 5.220
Heupferd 17.50
Herrenvolk 1.304; 2.224
Hestiasis 8.202
Heteira 1.154f
Heteros 8.118
Hieron 2.244, 336; 3.272f
Hilaskesthai 15.39
Hilasmos 15.38–40
Hilasterion 8.58
Himation 3.142

---

11 Phil, Col, Thes
12 Tim, Tit, Phlm
13 Heb
14 Jas, Pet
15 John, Jude
16 Rev, v.1
17 Rev, v.2

12.52; **14.**202
Kalupsis **16.**21
Kaluptesthai **1.**317
Kamelos **2.**217; **4.**229
Kamilos **2.**217; **4.**229
Kara **11.**26
Kartarizein **14.**273
Kartartismon **10.**149
Kartartizein **10.**149
Kata **6.**3; **8.**159
Katagraphein **6.**3
Katalalein **14.**111
Katalalia **9.**264; **14.**111, 190
Katalalos **8.**36
Katalambein **5.**49
Katanoein **13.**29
Katapausis **13.**35
Kataphilein **2.**335; **3.**345
Katastrophe **12.**172
Katatemnein **11.**55
Katergazesthai **11.**41
Katharizein **15.**30
Katharos **1.**105f; **10.**47; **12.**33f
Kathekonta **8.**33
Katheudein **1.**345
Katiasthai **14.**116
Katoikein **10.**132; **16.**91
Kauson **14.**47
Kenoun **11.**36
Kephas **2.**139
Kerugma **7.**22; **9.**25; **14.**140
Kerussein **1.**75, 362
Kerux **1.**75, 362; **12.**148;
 14.326
Khan **4.**21
Kethubah **12.**77
Kiddush **2.**202; **3.**337
Kinnor **4.**56
Kiomasthai **1.**345

Kleptes **3.**173
Kleronomia **14.**173
Kleros **14.**267f
Klopai **3.**173
Koimeterion **1.**345
Koinonia **9.**163
Koinonia pisteos **12.**278
Koinos **3.**164
Koite **8.**178
Kolakeia **11.**189
Kolaphizesthai **9.**40
Kollubistai **5.**110
Kollubos **5.**110
Kollurion **16.**138
Kolumban **5.**178
Kolumbethron **5.**178
Kombos **14.**270
Komos **8.**178; **10.**49
Kophinos **2.**126; **3.**158, 184;
 5.203
Kopian **8.**214; **11.**44f; **16.**62
Kopos **9.**215; **16.**62
Korban **2.**115f, 214f; **3.**8, 169–
 171; **6.**239
Korinthiazesthai **9.**2
Kosher **2.**112
Kosmios **12.**80f
Kosmos **6.**18; **14.**86f, 103;
 15.56, 105
Krabbatos **5.**180
Krasis **14.**58
Kraspedon **1.**346; **2.**286
Kratein **12.**189; **16.**61
Krauge **13.**47
Kretizein **12.**243
Krinein **11.**19
Krites **8.**35
Krustallon **16.**156
Kubeia **10.**151

Kuberneseis **9**.116
Kunaria **2**.122
Kuppah **7**.51; **12**.85
Kuria **15**.130, 138
Kurios **1**.248; **3**.298; **8**.11, 139,
  165; **9**.107; **10**.141; **11**.39;
  15.130; **17**.89, 138, 179
Kurios kai theos **16**.164
Kuriotes **14**.323
Kusi ballomena **11**.62

Lalein **13**.188
Lambanein **14**.62
Laos **9**.10; **16**.66
Lapis lazuli **17**.213
Lateinos **17**.101
Latreia **6**.190; **8**.156
Latreuein **8**.156
Latreuein kallei **8**.156f
Legatus **9**.209f
Legion **3**.118; **4**.108; **7**.79
Leipesthai **14**.44
Leitourgia **8**.202; **9**.164
Leitourgos **8**.202f; **11**.49f
Lepton **3**.302; **4**.171, 255
Lestes **3**.173; **4**.248
Lex talionis **1**.163
Libellus **1**.114
Liberalia **10**.34
Lictors **9**.184, 253
Lilin **3**.35
Lilith **1**.320; **3**.35
Limne **1**.76
Log **4**.155
Logia **8**.52; **9**.163; **14**.256
Logikos **14**.190
Logizesthai **9**.122
Logos **5**.7f, 35f, 56; **8**.113;
  11.117; **14**.191, 230

Logos akoes **15**.24
Logs **5**.249
Loidoresthai **9**.40
Lolium temulentum **2**.72
Loudaioi **5**.76
Louein **16**.34
Luein **16**.34
Lulabs **6**.116
Lumen Asiae **16**.58
Lutron **16**.177
Lutroun **10**.81
Lutrousthai **16**.177

Ma'ah **4**.241; **5**.109
Machai **14**.98
Magna est veritas et praevalebit
  2.377
Major domo **9**.36
Makarios **1**.89
Makrothumein **9**.119
Makrothumia **8**.42; **9**.216;
  10.50, 138; **11**.110, 158; **12**.196
Mal'akim **13**.17
Malakos **9**.52
Mamon **1**.249
Mancipatio **8**.106
Mandata dei **12**.127
Manthanontes **13**.52
Maran atha **9**.169; **14**.124
Marin **6**.247
Martha **15**.138
Martus **7**.13; **16**.92
Massah **13**.33
Mataiologoi **12**.241
Mataios **12**.241
Mathein **13**.48
Mathetes **6**.20
Mazzikin **3**.34
Mechitsah **1**.296

Megabyzi 15.124
Megalopsuchia 9.40
Melissae 12.67
Mellon aion 13.57
Memphesthai 11.60; 16.197
Mempsimoiros 15.197f
Memra 5.30
Menein 11.28
Mens sana in corpore sano
  12.119
Meribah 13.33
Merimna 1.255
Merimnan 1.255
Merismos 16.32
Mesites 13.89
Mesos 13.89
Messiah 10.107; 15.69; 17.60
Metamorphousthai 8.157
Metanoia 3.26; 13.53, 184
Methe 8.178
Methistemi 11.111
Methos 9.53
Methuskein 17.159
Metraloai 12.38
Metriopatheia 13.47
Metriopathein 13.46
Mezuzah 3.295
Miainein 14.173
Millenium 17.186
Mimesis 10.160
Min 5.213
Minah 4.172
Misanthropia 8.50
Miseria 6.4
Misericordia 6.4
Mnemonic 1.13
Moicheiai 3.173
Moira 15.197
Monai 6.153

Monogenes 5.74
Moriturus 8.85
Moros 1.140
Morphe 8.157f; 11.35–37
Mulos onikos 2.179
Mumcheh 5.110
Muopazon 14.306
Murex 17.160
Muscipula 2.235
Musterion 2.64; 3.92; 9.26;
  16.153; 17.143

Nai 16.37
Naos 2.243, 305, 336; 3.273
Neos 8.158; 9.189; 10.116;
  13.92; 16.98, 176
Neotes 12.98
Nephalios 12.79f, 247
Nephein 12.207; 14.252
Nephilum 14.322
Ne plus ultra 15.90
Neron 17.102
Nezer 1.40
Nikan 16.66
Nimbus 16.84
Nomen 8.212
Nomenclatores 17.163
Nomikos 12.266
Nominos 12.161
Nothros 13.49
Nouthetein 9.41
Nun aion 13.57

Odinai 16.7
Odium theologicum 2.34;
  12.162; 14.92
Ofanim 13.17
Oiketai 14.210
Oikiakoi 1.383

11 Phil, Col, Thes
12 Tim, Tit, Phlm
13 Heb
14 Jas, Pet
15 John, Jude
16 Rev, v.1
17 Rev, v.2

Praetor 8.106; 10.80
Praitorion 11.20
Praktor 1.145
Praotes 1.96; 10.51f, 137; 11.158
Prasiai 3.158
Praus 1.96; 10.52, 137f; 12.259
Prautes 9.238; 14.58
PRDS 10.41
Presbeutes 9.209f; 12.280
Presbuteros 12.70f; 15.127
Presbutes 12.280
Proagon 15.143
Prodotes 12.190
Prodromos 6.155; 13.63
Prographein 10.24f
Proi 5.88; 6.265f
Proistasthai 12.264
Prokope 11.20; 14.299
Prokoptein 11.20; 12.174
Prokoptontes 13.52
Propetes 12.191
Prosagein 14.235
Prosagoge 8.73; 14.235
Prosagogeus 10.117; 14.235
Prosechein 13.21
Proselutos 2.290
Proseuche 12.57
Proskunein 1.297
Prosopolempsia 14.62
Prosopon 14.62
Prosopon lambanein 14.62
Prosphiles 11.80
Prostasia 13.18
Pros thanaton 15.120
Proton 5.88
Prototokos 11.119; 16.32
Pseustai 12.39
Psithurismoi 9.264

Psithuristes 8.36
Psuche 9.28; 13.39; 14.93; 15.11, 166, 201
Psuchikos, oi 9.28; 14.93; 15.11f, 165f, 201f
Psuchros 16.141
Ptocheia 16.78
Ptochos 1.90
Ptoein 6.271
Ptossein 1.90
Publicanus 3.53
Pule 17.210
Pulon 17.210

Qolbon 2.245
Quadrans 4.171
Quahal 2.142
Quaternion 6.250; 7.95
Quelle 1.4
Qui cessat esse melior cessat esse bonus 13.52
Quo vadis? 13.58

Rabban 7.49
Rabbi 1.311; 6.269
Rabbounai 6.269
Raca 1.139
Raphis 7.2
Ratio marmorum 17.161
Recto 16.165
Rede 17.162
Religio licita 14.146, 156
Religiones (licitae et illicitae) 14.156
Remaz 10.41; 13.67
Renatus in aeternum 5.127; 17.33
Roizedon 14.344

Ruach 1.22, 49; 5.83, 131; 8.102

Ruparia 14.57

Rupos 14.57

Sacramentum 12.160; 14.245

Sagan 7.37

Sagene 1.78; 2.89; 3.27

Salaam 1.108

Salem 13.69

Sar 4.56

Sarkikos 9.29f

Sarkinoi 9.29f

Sarx, sarka 5.65; 8.101–103, 158; 9.29f, 239f

Satana 2.149f

Satraps 17.141, 147

Schema 8.157f; 11.35–37

Schismata 9.14

Scintilla 12.175; 15.79; 16.159

Scribo 15.50

Scrip 6.55

Seah 10.32

Sebaste 16.43

Sebastos 17.89, 138

Seiros 14.321

Seismos 1.317

Seleniazesthai 2.166

Semeion 5.9, 119

Semnos 11.79; 12.61, 236, 247

Semnotes 12.61f

Senate 12.70

Senechomai 11.27

Senex 12.70

Sepein 14.115

Serif 1.127; 4.211

Sesterces 9.249

Setobrotos 14.116

Shalom 1.108; 6.171; 10.9, 50, 76

Shechinah 2.161f; 5.69; 8.125; 14.259; 17.35f, 94, 202f

Shedim 1.320; 3.35; 9.92

Shekel 2.168; 4.172, 241; 5.109

Shekinah See Shechinah

Shema 1.192, 196; 2.278; 3.295; 17.119

Shomeron 6.31

Shomeroni 6.31

Shemoneh 'esreh 1.192f; 14.89f

Shoshben 5.143

Shub 1.52

Sicarii 2.332

Siloam 6.43

Sindon 3.141f

Siros 14.321

Skandalethron 1.148; 3.342

Skandalizein 2.170; 3.342

Skandalon 1.148; 2.170; 3.342; 4.215

Skene 17.35, 94, 202

Skenoun 17.35

Skia 13.112

Skleros 5.226

Skolops 9.257

Skotia 5.47

Skotos 5.47

Skubala 11.62

Sod 10.41; 13.67

Solam 17.50

Soluitur ambulando 12.171

Soma 14.93; 15.11, 201

Soma sema 12.175

Somatikos 11.95

Sophia 5.31; 9.109; 10.82f, 90; 11.108, 130; 14.295, 302

Sophron 12.80f, 239, 247, 251

Sophronein 14.251

Sophronismos 12.144f

11 Phil, Col, Thes
12 Tim, Tit, Phlm
13 Heb
14 Jas, Pet
15 John, Jude
16 Rev, v.1
17 Rev, v.2

13.26, 48, 52; 14.14, 61
Teleiotes 13.52
Teleioun 13.26, 48
Telos 1.177; 17.205
Tephillin 2.286
Tephra phrygia 16.139
Teras 5.119
Terma 12.11
Terumah 4.155; 9.80
Teshubah 1.52
Tesserae 16.96
Tetelestai 2.369; 6.258
Tetrachelismenos 13.40
Tetragrammaton 6.210; 17.180
Tetrarch 2.95; 4.31
Tetuphomenos 12.191
Thalassa 1.76; 5.208; 16.41
Thanatos 17.9
Theasthai 5.64; 15.23
Theion, s 1.119; 17.138
Themelioun 14.274
Theologos 16.13
Theos 5.39; 7.2; 12.50, 138
Theostugeis 8.36f
Thlipsis 8.73; 9.170, 213;
    16.40, 78
Threskia 14.61
Thuia articulata 17.160
Thumos 1.138; 9.264; 10.159;
    11.153; 12.236
Timan 12.138
Time 12.50; 14.291
Tittle 1.85, 127
Toga 10.34
Tolman 14.329
Tolmetes 14.329
Torah 3.31f
Trierarchia 8.202

Trimita 16.138
Triremes 9.3, 36
Trochos geneseos 14.87
Trope 14.54
Truphein 14.119
Tsaraath 3.44
Tupos 14.244
Tzedakah 1.187
Tzelatzel 17.51

Urbs candida 16.122

Vehemens 14.252
Verso 16.165f
Vilicus 14.255
Vilis 11.69
Vindicatio 8.106

Xenos 10.118; 13.148; 15.149

Yada 11.63
Yashmak 9.97
Yetzer hara 8.98; 14.50
Yetzer hatob 8.98; 14.50

Zadik 1.57
Zanah 2.73
Zelos 8.179; 9.263f; 10.47;
    14.91, 104
Zelotes 1.359; 14.229
Zen 5.43
Zestos 16.141
Ziz 6.228f
Zizanium 2.73
Zizith 1.346; 2.286
Zoe 5.43
Zugon 8.55
Zunim 2.73

---

11 Phil, Col, Thes   13 Heb   15 John, Jude   16 Rev, v.1
12 Tim, Tit, Phlm   14 Jas, Pet   17 Rev, v.2

INDEX OF ANCIENT WRITINGS